Ancient Egypt: A Very Short Introduction

VERY SHORT INTRODUCTIONS are for anyone wanting a stimulating and accessible way into a new subject. They are written by experts, and have been translated into more than 45 different languages.

The series began in 1995, and now covers a wide variety of topics in every discipline. The VSI library currently contains over 650 volumes—a Very Short Introduction to everything from Psychology and Philosophy of Science to American History and Relativity—and continues to grow in every subject area.

Very Short Introductions available now:

ABOLITIONISM Richard S. Newman
THE ABRAHAMIC RELIGIONS
    Charles L. Cohen
ACCOUNTING Christopher Nobes
ADAM SMITH Christopher J. Berry
ADOLESCENCE Peter K. Smith
ADVERTISING Winston Fletcher
AERIAL WARFARE Frank Ledwidge
AESTHETICS Bence Nanay
AFRICAN AMERICAN RELIGION
    Eddie S. Glaude Jr
AFRICAN HISTORY John Parker and
    Richard Rathbone
AFRICAN POLITICS Ian Taylor
AFRICAN RELIGIONS
    Jacob K. Olupona
AGEING Nancy A. Pachana
AGNOSTICISM Robin Le Poidevin
AGRICULTURE Paul Brassley and
    Richard Soffe
ALBERT CAMUS Oliver Gloag
ALEXANDER THE GREAT
    Hugh Bowden
ALGEBRA Peter M. Higgins
AMERICAN BUSINESS HISTORY
    Walter A. Friedman
AMERICAN CULTURAL HISTORY
    Eric Avila
AMERICAN FOREIGN RELATIONS
    Andrew Preston
AMERICAN HISTORY Paul S. Boyer
AMERICAN IMMIGRATION
    David A. Gerber
AMERICAN LEGAL HISTORY
    G. Edward White

AMERICAN MILITARY HISTORY
    Joseph T. Glatthaar
AMERICAN NAVAL HISTORY
    Craig L. Symonds
AMERICAN POLITICAL HISTORY
    Donald Critchlow
AMERICAN POLITICAL PARTIES
    AND ELECTIONS L. Sandy Maisel
AMERICAN POLITICS
    Richard M. Valelly
THE AMERICAN PRESIDENCY
    Charles O. Jones
THE AMERICAN REVOLUTION
    Robert J. Allison
AMERICAN SLAVERY
    Heather Andrea Williams
THE AMERICAN WEST Stephen Aron
AMERICAN WOMEN'S HISTORY
    Susan Ware
ANAESTHESIA Aidan O'Donnell
ANALYTIC PHILOSOPHY
    Michael Beaney
ANARCHISM Colin Ward
ANCIENT ASSYRIA Karen Radner
ANCIENT EGYPT Ian Shaw
ANCIENT EGYPTIAN ART AND
    ARCHITECTURE Christina Riggs
ANCIENT GREECE Paul Cartledge
THE ANCIENT NEAR EAST
    Amanda H. Podany
ANCIENT PHILOSOPHY Julia Annas
ANCIENT WARFARE
    Harry Sidebottom
ANGELS David Albert Jones
ANGLICANISM Mark Chapman

Ian Shaw

ANCIENT EGYPT

A Very Short Introduction
SECOND EDITION

OXFORD
UNIVERSITY PRESS

OXFORD
UNIVERSITY PRESS

Great Clarendon Street, Oxford, OX2 6DP,
United Kingdom

Oxford University Press is a department of the University of Oxford.
It furthers the University's objective of excellence in research, scholarship,
and education by publishing worldwide. Oxford is a registered trade mark of
Oxford University Press in the UK and in certain other countries

© Ian Shaw 2021

The moral rights of the author have been asserted

First edition published 2004
This edition published 2021

Published in the United States of America by Oxford University Press
198 Madison Avenue, New York, NY 10016, United States of America

British Library Cataloguing in Publication Data
Data available

Library of Congress Control Number: 2020943340

ISBN 978-0-19-884546-1

Printed and bound by
CPI Group (UK) Ltd, Croydon, CR0 4YY

To my amazing daughters Nia and Elin

Contents

Preface

One way of understanding an ancient culture is to immerse ourselves in the surviving evidence, and in the case of Egypt there is obviously no shortage of such material, from coffins, tombs, painted temples, myths, and prayers, through to some of the humble domestic paraphernalia of day-to-day life. But if we are seeking to gain real insights into the past, we need to know how all of these aspects of ancient Egyptian culture were discovered and documented (and, in the case of objects, frequently removed from their original contexts). We also need to see how our views of them have been coloured not only by the long procession of scholars who have found and interpreted the places, objects, and texts, but also by modern attempts to transform all this intriguing stuff into art, fiction, documentaries, and entertainment. This *Very Short Introduction to Ancient Egypt* therefore seeks insights from Egyptology (and occasionally pseudo-Egyptology) as a way of accessing the elusive nature of ancient Egypt itself.

Ancient Egyptian culture—as a well-defined phenomenon expressed in highly distinctive physical forms and speaking to us in various ways, through a unique set of scripts—has a kind of poignant, visible end point. In the temple of the goddess Isis on the island of Philae, a few miles to the south of the city of Aswan, one wall bears a brief hieroglyphic inscription. Its significance is not in its content or meaning but purely in its date—it was written on 24 August AD 394, making this the last recorded day on which we definitely know that the hieroglyphic script was used. The *language* of ancient Egypt survived considerably longer (Philae temple also contains the last graffiti in the more cursive 'demotic' script, dating to 2 December AD 452), and in a sense it still exists in fossilized form in the liturgical texts of the modern Coptic Church. Nevertheless, it was around the end of the 4th century AD that the knowledge and use of hieroglyphs effectively vanished. Until the decipherment of hieroglyphs by Jean-François Champollion in 1822, the written world of the Egyptians remained hidden, and scholars were almost entirely reliant on the accounts left by Greek and Roman authors, or the sections of the Bible story in which Egypt features. Classical and biblical images of Egypt therefore dominated the emerging subject of Egyptology until almost the end of the 19th century.

More than 180 years after Champollion's breakthrough, the study of ancient Egypt has influenced and permeated a vast number of contemporary issues, from linguistics and 'Afrocentrism' to religious cults and bizarre theories involving extraterrestrials. This book combines discussion of the archaeological and historical study of ancient Egypt with appraisal of the impact of Egypt—and its many icons—on past and present Western society and thought. It is intended both to give the reader a sense of some of the crucial issues that dominate the modern study of ancient Egypt, and also to attempt to discuss some of the reasons why the culture of the Egyptians is still so appealing and fascinating to us.

As in the first edition of this book, much of the discussion focuses, initially at least, on the 'Narmer Palette' (*c.*3100 BC), outlining its significance with regard to our understanding of early Egyptian culture. Each chapter then takes a different aspect of the palette as a starting point for consideration of key aspects of ancient Egypt, such as history, writing, religion, and funerary beliefs. Within this structure, current Egyptological ideas and discoveries are discussed, and sometimes contextualized with more populist and commercial viewpoints, including ancient Egypt's widespread exploitation by modern mass media. In the last fifteen years, there have been many developments in cultural heritage and museums in Egypt—Chapter 10 is therefore an entirely new section, discussing, among other things, the archaeological and cultural implications of rapid and significant political change since the so-called Arab Spring in 2011, via the short-lived government of Mohammed Morsi, and through to the current regime of Abdel Fattah el-Sisi.

Acknowledgements

I would like to thank George Miller for commissioning the first
edition of this *Very Short Introduction*, and Jenny Nugée for
suggesting this revised version. For important insights that
contributed both to the section on the Wadi Hammamat quarries
and to the new chapter dealing with recent developments in
cultural heritage management in Egypt, and for numerous highly
productive (and occasionally quite heated) discussions on ancient
Egypt and archaeology, many of which have enhanced this revised
edition, I am eternally grateful to my wife Dr Elizabeth Bloxam.
I am also grateful to an anonymous external reviewer for some
very helpful suggestions and corrections.

List of illustrations

Ancient Egypt

The publisher and the author apologize for any errors or omissions in the above list. If contacted they will be pleased to rectify these at the earliest opportunity.

Chapter 1
Introduction

In 1898 the British Egyptologists James Quibell and Frederick
Green uncovered a sculpted slab of greywacke (a greenish-grey
slate-like stone) in the ruins of an early temple at the Upper
Egyptian site of Hierakonpolis. Unlike the discovery of
Tutankhamun's tomb twenty-four years later, this find would not
bring the world's journalists racing to the scene, but its discoverers
were almost immediately aware of its importance. Like the
Rosetta Stone, this carved slab—the Narmer Palette—would have
powerful repercussions for the study of ancient Egypt, spreading
far beyond its immediate significance at Hierakonpolis. For the
next century or so, it would be variously interpreted by
Egyptologists attempting to solve numerous different problems,
from the political origins of the Egyptian state to the nature of
Egyptian art and writing. No single object can necessarily typify
an entire culture, but the Narmer Palette is one of a few surviving
artefacts from the Nile Valley that are so iconic and so rich in
information that they can act as microcosms of certain aspects of
ancient Egyptian culture as a whole.

The Narmer Palette

The Narmer Palette is a shield-shaped slab of greywacke, 63 cm
high, with carved low-relief decoration on both faces, and it is

1

1a. Front view of the Narmer Palette (Cairo, Egyptian Museum), **c.3000 BC.**

usually dated to the final century of the 4th millennium BC. On the front, there is a depiction of intertwined long-necked lions ('serpopards') held on leashes by two bearded men. Symmetrical pairs of 'tamed' beasts such as these seem to be adapted from early

1*b*. Back view of the Narmer Palette, *c.*3000 BC.

Mesopotamian, perhaps Elamite, iconography. In an Egyptian context, however, they may specifically represent the enforced unification of the two halves of the country, which is a theme in Egyptian art and texts throughout the pharaonic period.

The circle formed by the entwining necks of the serpopards ingeniously creates the depression or saucer in which pigments for eye-paint might have been crushed (the original purpose of these palettes), but it is unclear whether such significant ceremonial artefacts as the Narmer Palette were ever actually used for this function. Highly charged ritual objects such as these perhaps transcended the supposed function of the thing itself, as they took on the role of offerings dedicated to the Hierakonpolis temple. On other ceremonial palettes of similar type, the circular depression can have the unwanted effect of interrupting the smooth flow of the scenes depicted. Compare, for instance, the 'Two-dog Palette', also excavated by Quibell and Green at Hierakonpolis, where there are once again two long-necked lions on the front, but the depression simply sits between the necks rather than being created by them (or the 'Battlefield Palette', where the depression interrupts a row of captives).

In the top register on the front of the palette, above the two serpopards, the artist has carved the striding bearded figure of an early Egyptian ruler, probably identified as a man called Narmer, judging by the hieroglyphs both in front of him and in the *serekh* frame in the centre of the top of the palette, between the two cow's heads. He is shown wearing the so-called Red Crown, which is first attested on a potsherd dating to the Naqada I period (*c.*3800–3600 BC) and eventually became connected with the control of Lower Egypt (but whether it had yet developed this association in Naqada I, or even in the reign of Narmer, is uncertain). He is also carrying a mace and a flail, and wearing a tunic tied over his left shoulder, with a bull's tail hanging from the waist.

The king is taking part in a procession with six other people, including two figures about half his size, who are situated behind and in front of him on the palette, but are perhaps intended to be regarded as walking on either side of him in reality. These two men, both clean-shaven, evidently represent high officials. The one to the left is clearly a 'sandal-bearer' (an actual title held by some eminent royal officials in later times), since he carries a pair of sandals in one hand and a small vessel in the other, while a pectoral, or perhaps royal seal, is tied around his neck by a cord. A single hieroglyph in a rectangular frame or box is placed behind and above his head; this sign, perhaps being a representation of a reed 'float', like those used by Old Kingdom hunters of hippopotami (but of uncertain meaning in this context), is usually rendered phonetically as *db3*. He also has two different signs hovering in front of his head, apparently a superimposed rosette sign and the *ḥm* sign that later came to have several meanings, including 'servant'. The official to the right is represented at a slightly larger scale, and is shown wearing a wig and a leopard-skin costume, as well as possibly writing equipment slung around his neck. He may be identified by two hieroglyphs above his head spelling the word *tt*, perhaps an early version of the word for vizier.

The king and these two officials, along with four smaller standard-bearers (all but one of whom are shown bearded), are evidently reviewing the decapitated and castrated bodies of ten of their enemies. These corpses are laid out on the far right, each with his head between his legs, and all but one with the severed phallus of the deceased placed on his head. This review of the enemy dead is presumably in the aftermath of a battle or an act of ritual slaughter. The four standards are topped by symbols or totems which are known from later periods, comprising two falcons, one jackal (perhaps the god Wepwawet), and a strange globular item that is clearly the *šdšd* or royal placenta. These standards, taken together, form a group that were later identified as the so-called 'followers of Horus' (or 'the gods who follow Horus'), who had strong associations with the celebration of a royal jubilee or funeral. Above the corpses are four signs or images: a door, a falcon, a boat with high prow and stern, and a falcon holding a harpoon.

On the other side of the palette is a much larger, muscular, striding figure of Narmer, this time shown wearing the conical White Crown of Upper Egypt along with the same tunic tied over his left shoulder and the bull's tail hanging from his waist, as well as fringes ending in cow's heads. On this occasion he is accompanied only by the sandal-bearer (behind him, or to one side, depending on how we interpret the use of perspective here), while he smites an enemy with a pear-shaped mace held up above his head. The mace is held slightly oddly, halfway up the handle. The sandal-bearer is again shown at just under half the size of the king, although the ruler's tall crown makes him tower even more over the rest of the figures in the scene. Once more, the sandal-bearer has the rosette and *ḥm* signs by his head. The king is gripping the hair of the captive (whose facial features seem Egyptian rather than Libyan or Asiatic), and the latter has two ideograms floating to the right of his head. These two small images are presumed by most Egyptologists to be the early hieroglyphs for 'harpoon' (*wꜥ*) and 'lake' (*š*), which would either phonetically spell out the foreign name 'Wash', or refer to someone whose name, title, or even place of origin was actually 'Harpoon-lake'. It seems likely that the falcon holding a harpoon, depicted as one of the group of enigmatic signs above the decapitated bodies on the front of the palette (see above) is also communicating the idea of the defeat of Wash/Harpoon by the king in the guise of the Horus-falcon.

In front of the king, and above the captive, the falcon-god Horus hovers, holding a schematically rendered captive by a rope attached to the man's nose. This captive has six papyri protruding from his back, and it has been suggested that this identifies the rebus as '6,000 captives', on the basis that each of the papyrus plants already signifies the number 1,000 as they later would in the pharaonic period. An alternative reading is that this group of plants is an iconographical reference to the homeland of the captive, which might have been the papyrus-filled land of northern Egypt. It is possible that the 'harpoon' and 'lake' signs

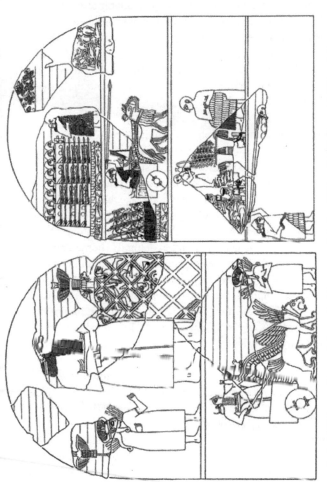

2. Stele of Vultures (Louvre), from the Mesopotamian city of Girsu (Early Dynastic III period, c.2560 BC), showing the local god, Ningirsu, wielding a mace over naked enemies trapped in a net.

may be intended to refer to the king's captive as well as to the one held by the falcon, so that both may actually be the same person/people. In the lowest section of this side of the palette are two prone naked human figures, who are presumably also intended to be either captives or dead enemies. Each of these has a sign to the left of his face (see Chapter 6 for the possible meaning of these signs) and both of their bodies are twisted so that their faces are pointing leftwards, i.e. in the same direction as the two captives above, and in the opposite direction to the king and the sandal-bearer.

The visual appearance and the very complex content of the Narmer Palette's decoration have been the subject of constant discussion ever since its discovery. The style of the images and the identification of the king as Narmer demonstrate that it was created at the end of the 4th millennium BC, when many of the most distinctive elements of Egyptian culture were emerging, and Egypt was essentially moving from prehistory to history. The images already incorporate a number of highly characteristic features of pharaonic art, such as the arrangement of the picture into a series of horizontal 'registers', the semi-diagrammatic depiction of people and animals as a combination of frontal and sideways elements, and the use of size as a means of indicating each individual's relative importance. The latter is very much the iconography of power.

In a cross-cultural study of the palette, the Canadian archaeologist Bruce Trigger points out that the specific 'Egyptianness' of the smiting scene can be counterbalanced by various aspects of the iconography that seem to be universal. Noting the obvious contrast between the king's elaborate regalia and his virtually naked victim, he cites the Stele of Vultures, excavated from the ancient Mesopotamian city of Girsu, and now in the Louvre (Early Dynastic III period, *c*.2560 BC), on which the local god Ningirsu wields a mace over a group of naked enemies trapped in a net. In a further parallel to the Narmer Palette's iconography, the other side of this stele portrays Eannatum, the *ensi* (ruler) of Lagash trampling defeated enemies underfoot, while vultures devour their severed heads. Trigger also makes a fascinating comparison with a Maya scene on a carved lintel from Yaxchilan, showing a ruler called Bird-Jaguar capturing two of his enemies (*c.*AD 755). In the Maya scene, the richly clothed triumphant warriors contrast with the semi-naked defeated rulers, one of whom is held by his hair. As Trigger concludes,

> Although the scene on the Narmer palette does not necessarily depict the capture in battle of an adversary, the psychological affinities between these two representations are very close, notwithstanding their having evolved wholly independently of one another, in different hemispheres, and far removed in time.

This comment might be applied in some respects to Egyptian culture as a whole, where we find ourselves constantly veering between the thought that 'they're just like us' and the alternative view that they are also very peculiarly and distinctively Egyptian. As Barry Kemp says, in *Ancient Egypt: Anatomy of a Civilisation* (much recommended as a longer introduction to ancient Egypt),

> I am trying to be an objective observer, examining evidence from ancient Egypt as if I were a botanist looking at species of ferns. Yet I can only make sense of the evidence by accepting that I myself am part of it, and how I join up the fragments depends on the fact that I am human, too, living within my own cultural sphere. There is no clear and absolute answer as to where the line should be drawn between too much empathy and too little.

If the attraction of ancient Egyptian culture is its combination of exotica and familiarity, the role of the Egyptologist seems to be to use the available archaeological, visual, and textual sources to distinguish between, on the one hand, aspects of life that are culturally specific either to ourselves or to the ancient Egyptians and, on the other hand, key characteristics of humanity and behaviour that transcend place and time. This is of course not the only reason for studying the civilization of ancient Egypt, although it is this kind of mindset that constantly challenges us to view Egypt not in isolation but as one of many human cultural responses to particular environmental and historical conditions.

What is ancient Egypt?

The earliest known 'Egyptians'—if we can call them this before Egypt existed as a cultural or ethnic phenomenon—are attested in Palaeolithic north-eastern Africa in *c*.400,000 BC. The first evidence of tools takes the form of large stone hand-axes, but the earliest actual human remains (the body of a child found at Taramsa Hill in southern Egypt) are about 55,000 years old. Between these two dates (i.e. 400,000–55,000 BC) Egypt passed through the long Lower and Middle Palaeolithic periods of human prehistory. The presence of early 'hominins' (initially *Homo erectus* and later *Homo sapiens*) is attested by scattered stone toolkits surviving in the eastern part of the Sahara now occupied by Egypt. These hunter-gatherers survived through long periods of hyperaridity, alternating with much shorter phases when wetter conditions prevailed. For example, stratified deposits at the site of Sodmein Cave, located in the central Eastern desert, show occupation from the Middle Palaeolithic to the Neolithic. During the Mesolithic period (*c*.10,000–5000 BC) a number of semi-nomadic cultures inhabited the immediate area of the Nile Valley, relying on hunting and fishing for their subsistence. Finally, from about 6000 BC onwards, the climate of northeastern Africa became gradually wetter, encouraging the development of more settled communities along the Nile, primarily relying on animal and plant domestication. Excavation of these semi-permanent settlements, such as Wadi Kubbaniya, in the Aswan region, have revealed intensive evidence of plant processing in many domestic settings.

By the beginning of the 4th millennium BC, settled communities had emerged at the northern end of the Nile Valley. Rainfall was (and still is) very low throughout the region, so the rich agricultural land of Egypt was watered by the river's annual flooding (or 'indundation'), which deposited new layers of fertile silt along the riverbanks. The strips of cultivated land vary in thickness on either side, as the river meanders northwards. The River Nile, stretching from its sources in eastern and central Africa down to the Mediterranean coast, is therefore the single most important element in the geography of Egypt. Egyptologists tend to divide the country into two sections, largely derived from textual sources: first Upper Egypt, the southern part, consisting of the land from Wadi Halfa to Cairo, and second Lower Egypt, in the north, where the Nile fans out into several branches, forming a large and fertile delta, before disgorging into the Mediterranean. The textual sources also suggest that ancient Egyptians called their country Kemet ('black land', referring to the black fertile soil), in contrast to the surrounding Deshret ('red land' or desert). Within this geographical setting, a sophisticated culture steadily emerged.

The archaeology of pharaonic Egypt spans three millennia (c.3100–332 BC) and encompasses a diverse body of artefacts, architecture, texts, and organic remains. Museums throughout the world contain millions of Egyptian antiquities, and an even greater number of remains are still *in situ* in the Nile Valley and the Delta, ranging from temples, tombs, and cities to remote rock inscriptions carved on crags in the Libyan Desert, the Eastern Desert, or the Sinai peninsula. Three principal factors have facilitated the survival of an unusual wealth of detail concerning pharaonic Egypt: first, an elite group's penchant for grandiose and elaborate funerary arrangements, second, suitably arid conditions of preservation, and finally the use of writing on a wide variety of media.

The history of the rediscovery of ancient Egypt is in many respects the same as that of any other early civilization, in that centuries of ignorance and plundering were gradually replaced by the more enlightened approaches of late 19th-century and 20th-century scholars. Within this broad trend, however, various specific aspects of the study of ancient Egypt—such as epigraphy, excavation, philology, and anthropology—have progressed at very different rates.

Greek and Roman views of Egypt

The first people from outside Egypt to show interest in studying the Egyptians as a unique and fascinating anthropological phenomenon were the ancient Greeks. Although archaeological evidence in Egypt and elsewhere shows that there were commercial contacts between Egyptians and Greeks from at least the late 3rd millennium BC, it was recruitment of large numbers of Greek mercenary soldiers by the 26th-Dynasty ruler Psamtek I, in the 7th century BC, that probably marked the beginning of full-scale contact between the two civilizations.

Between the 5th century BC and the 2nd century AD, numerous Greek and Roman scholars visited Egypt, and the accounts that they gave of their visits provide our first real verbal and intellectual view of Egypt from the outside. Sadly, however, the works of many ancient writers on Egypt have not survived—one major reason for this was the burning of the library at Alexandria in 47 BC and then again in AD 391, when 700,000 works, including Manetho's 36-volume history of Egypt (see Chapter 3 below), were lost.

The best-known, and most informative, ancient Greek visitor to Egypt was of course Herodotus of Halicarnassus, the traveller and historian. His nine volumes of *Histories* were written between 430 and 425 BC, and the second book is entirely devoted to Egypt. Herodotus is the earliest major textual source of information on mummification and other ancient Egyptian religious and funerary customs, and he attracted numerous later imitators, including Strabo and Diodorus Siculus. His travels in Egypt may have extended as far south as Aswan, but he gives no detailed account of Thebes, concentrating mainly on places in Lower Egypt. He seems to have relied mainly on rather low-ranking Egyptian priests for his evidence, but his astute observations included the identification of the pyramids as royal burial places. Herodotus not only provides a great deal of ethnographic information on 5th-century Egypt, but also gives us a version of Egyptian history for about 200 years of the Late Period, from the reign of Psamtek I, c.650 BC to the date that Herodotus visited Egypt, c.450 BC (by which time Egypt had become a satrapy in the Persian Empire). Occasionally archaeological work has shown Herodotus' descriptions to be surprisingly accurate, as in the case of Tell Basta, the site of the temple and town of Bubastis, in the eastern Nile Delta, about 80 km to the north-east of Cairo. In 1887–9, Édouard Naville's excavation of the main monument at the site, the red granite temple of the cat-goddess Bastet, confirmed many of the architectural details of the Greek historian's report.

Indigenous Egyptian texts of the 5th century BC, although quite extensive, are to a large extent full of stereotyped, obsolescent material that cannot be regarded as reliable in modern historical terms. Herodotus, however, is not without his own problems, and arguably presents a view of Egyptian history that has been deliberately fashioned to suit Greek tastes and ideas. Not only that, but it was demonstrated in 1887 by the German philologist Herman Diels that Herodotus was extensively plagiarizing the work of his illustrious predecessor Hecataeus of Miletus, who is known to have visited Egypt in about 500 BC. It has consequently been argued that Hecataeus deserves at least some of the credit for developing the basic intellectual framework that characterized Herodotus and most later Greek authors writing about Egypt.

Some Greeks were in the Nile Valley purely for commercial or military reasons (or just passing through), and these individuals have left behind some of the earliest tourist and 'pilgrimage' graffiti on the sights and monuments that they visited. One of the best collections of this kind of graffiti is on the northernmost of the Colossi of Memnon, two colossal statues that stand in front of the remains of the 18th-Dynasty mortuary temple of Amenhotep III, on the west bank at Thebes. The Greeks knew the statue as the 'vocal Memnon', interpreting the unusual whistling noise it made each morning as the Homeric character Memnon singing to his mother Eos, goddess of the dawn. Even in the remote 19th-Dynasty temples of Ramesses II down at Abu Simbel in Nubia there are graffiti left by Carian, Greek, and Phoenician soldiers who formed part of Psamtek II's expedition against the Kushites in the early 6th century BC. The Greek historian Strabo, who spent several years at Alexandria in the late 1st century BC, discusses several of the Theban monuments, including the Colossi and the New Kingdom rock-tombs. Although not generally as informative as the work of Herodotus, and considerably more prone to patronizing remarks concerning Egyptian culture, Strabo's *Geography* is nevertheless a valuable record of Egypt in the 1st century BC.

Herodotus and his successors provide us with information about Egypt in the Late Period and Greco-Roman times, but they also help to give us a sense of the intellectual and spiritual concerns of Egyptians. Although the Greek and Roman writers frequently seem to have been wrong in their assessment of the Egyptians' religion and philosophy, their reactions often involve the same kind of complex mixture of responses that are evoked in many modern researchers.

The Bible and Egypt

There can be no doubting the presence of Greeks and Romans in Egypt, but attempts to correlate biblical narratives with the

Egyptian textual and archaeological record have often been distinctly problematic. Most scholars' efforts to assign precise dates to biblical episodes involving Egypt tend to be thwarted by the uncertainty of the chronological background of the Old Testament. It also seems likely that many events of great significance to the Israelites cannot be assumed to have had the same importance for the ancient Egyptians, therefore there is no guarantee of any independent Egyptian record having been made, let alone being one of the very small proportion of texts that have actually survived.

Definite datable references to Egypt do not seem to appear in the Bible until the 1st millennium BC, when there are a number of specific allusions to the Egyptians, particularly in connection with battles against the Assyrians and Persians. It may have been during the reign of the 21st-Dynasty ruler 'Osorkon the elder', c.980 BC, that Hadad the Edomite (an adversary of Solomon, who is mentioned in 1 Kings 11), stayed in Egypt. The 22nd-Dynasty ruler Shoshenq I (945–924 BC) is almost certainly the biblical Shishak, who is said to have pillaged Jerusalem and the temple of Solomon in 925 BC. About two centuries later, the Egyptian prince Tefnakht of Sais, is alleged to have been the 'So, King of Egypt' contacted by Hosea, the ruler of Samaria, when he was looking for military aid in his struggles against an Assyrian invasion (2 Kings 17).

However, these very specific references to named rulers are highly exceptional cases, and generally speaking provable links between ancient Egypt and the Old Testament narrative are controversial and heavily debated. Since most of the events described in the Bible occurred several hundred years before the time that they were written down, it is extremely difficult to know when they are factual historical accounts and when they are purely allegorical or rhetorical in nature. Further potential problems occur because of anachronistic Egyptian names, places, or cultural phenomena that may belong not to the time when the events are supposed to have happened, but to later periods when the texts were actually written down. This may be the case, for instance, with the story of Joseph (Genesis 37–50), which is usually assumed to have taken place in the New Kingdom (1550–1070 BC) but contains certain details that tie in much more with the Egyptian political situation of the Saite period (664–525 BC).

Probably the most frequently discussed biblical link with Egypt is the Exodus story. There is a popular assumption that Ramesses II (whose overall reputation is discussed in Chapter 5) was the pharaoh involved in the expulsion of the Israelites from Egypt. The evidence linking Ramesses specifically with the Exodus story is fairly slim, hinging partly on the statement, in *Exodus I*: 11, that the enslaved Israelites were put to work at the cities of 'Pithom and Ramesses', the latter perhaps to be identified with Piramesse, a site founded by Ramesses and his father in the eastern Delta. It has also been pointed out that Ramesses' eldest son, Amunherkhepeshef appears to vanish from the records fairly early in his father's reign, leading some scholars to suggest that he might have died young and thus might be a theoretical candidate for pharaoh's slaughtered 'firstborn' in the Exodus narrative. However, Farouk Gomaa argues that this son might simply have changed his name to Amunherwenemef or Sethherkhepeshef, both of which continue to appear in texts until fairly late in Ramesses' reign. If Gomaa is correct, this particular son would therefore still be alive in the fortieth year of Ramesses II's reign, thus suggesting that he was perhaps in his fifties when he died, making him a much less plausible candidate for the slaughtered firstborn.

Sadly Gomaa was about half a century too late to prevent Cecil B. DeMille from casting Ramesses as the villain in his celebrated silent movie *The Ten Commandments* (1923). The same applies to the 1990s Dreamworks Exodus-set animation, *Prince of Egypt*, and Ridley Scott's *Exodus; Gods and Kings*, released in 2014, in both of which Ramesses was once again in the hot seat.

Some Egyptologists have suggested that the 'pharaoh' of the Exodus was actually Ramesses' son and successor Merenptah, partly on the basis of a 'victory stele' from the latter's reign that is the earliest document of any kind to mention Israel. Dating to the fifth year of his reign (c.1208), it consists of a series of hymns celebrating Merenptah's victories over various foreign enemies. Among the Palestinian enemies is the word Israel, significantly accompanied by a hieroglyph that indicates a people rather than a town or geographical area:

> Plundered is Canaan with every evil; carried off is Ashkelon; seized upon is Gezer; Yanoam is made as that which does not exist; Israel is laid waste, his seed is not; Hurru has become a widow for Egypt. All lands together, they are pacified.

However, as this translated extract shows, the stele actually tells us very little about the origins or nature of Israel, and certainly makes no reference to the presence of Israelites in Egypt, let alone their expulsion. In fact Merenptah's stele may not even be the earliest Egyptian reference to Israel, as an inscription on a fragment of an 18th-Dynasty statue pedestal in Berlin seems to mention Israel as an ethnic group nearly two centuries earlier.

Queen Hatshepsut, in the early 18th Dynasty, has also been suggested as the Exodus pharaoh, on the somewhat dubious grounds that the parting of the waters of the Red Sea could then be explained as a result of the volcanic eruption on the island of Santorini in the Aegean, which was thought to coincide with her reign. However, most recent estimates of the date of the Santorini eruption set it at c.1620, about 150 years before Hatshepsut's reign.

The Canadian Egyptologist Donald Redford argues more radically that the Exodus account is simply a mishmash of stories which probably originated in distant memories of the expulsion of the Hyksos (the Asiatic kings who ruled northern Egypt during the Second Intermediate Period). In *Moses the Egyptian*, Jan Assmann suggests that it represents not only a folk memory of the end of the Hyksos period, when Egypt expelled Asiatic rulers from northern Egypt, but perhaps also a kind of mythologization of the so-called 'heretical' Amarna period (for more on which, see Chapter 9). He concludes that the Exodus story is ultimately to be regarded as a convenient use of such folk tales to allow the Israelites to define themselves as a distinct nation.

An intriguing direct literary (and perhaps religious) link between Egypt and the Bible is the so-called Hymn to the Aten (the longest version of which was found in the tomb of Aye at Amarna), which is very similar in style and content to Psalm 104. This hymn is said to have been composed by the pharaoh Akhenaten, who is credited with transforming Egyptian religion into a single cult, based around the sun-disc deity Aten, which is considered by some to be monotheistic. Attempts have occasionally been made to equate Akhenaten with Moses (including Sigmund Freud's book: *Moses and Monotheism*). However, there are no other aspects of this pharaoh's life, or indeed his Atenist cult, that resemble the biblical account of Moses. The similarities with the psalm probably result only from the fact that the two compositions share a common literary heritage—they may even both derive from a common Near Eastern original. The same reason is usually given for the very close parallels that have been observed between a Late Period wisdom text known as the *Instruction of Amenemipet son of Kanakht* and the biblical book of Proverbs, although it has been suggested by some scholars that the writers of Proverbs may even have been influenced by a text of the *Instruction of Amenemipet* itself.

It is an irony of biblical archaeology that the more we investigate the texts and archaeological remains that link Egypt with the Bible, the less substantial and the less convincing these kinds of connections appear to be. As John Romer observed in *Testament:*

The Bible and History: 'Ultimately archaeology can neither "prove" nor "disprove" the Old Testament, only modern theories about what it might mean.' The biblical archaeology of Egypt was perhaps always doomed to be something of a blind alley, but undoubtedly in the early years of Egyptology both classical and biblical writings played the crucial role of familiar routes into an otherwise alien and largely incomprehensible landscape.

The emergence of 'Egyptology'

As with the question of the date at which European antiquarianism was superseded by archaeology, it is not easy to suggest a specific date when the writings of 'early travellers' and the collecting of Egyptian antiquities became transformed into something approaching the modern discipline of Egyptology. Most histories of Egyptian archaeology, however, see the Napoleonic expedition at the beginning of the 19th century as the first systematic attempt to record and describe the standing remains of pharaonic Egypt. The importance of the *Description de l'Égypte* –the multi-volume publication that resulted from the expedition—lay not only in its high standards of draughtsmanship and accuracy but also in the fact that it constituted a continuous and internally consistent appraisal by a single group of scholars, thus providing the first real attempt at an assessment of ancient Egypt in its entirety.

Despite the scientific aims of Napoleon's 'savants', virtually all 19th-century excavations in Egypt were designed to provide art treasures for European and American museums and private collections, since the expeditions' financial support invariably derived from these sources. What is remarkable about the European expeditions to Egypt in the first half of the 19th century is the rapid pace with which new information was acquired, digested, and assimilated into the overall picture of the pharaonic period. In 1838 the French architect Hector Horeau published a 'panorama' of Egypt including an illustration showing the

3. Major archaeological sites in Egypt mentioned in the text.

principal monuments of Egypt. The painting took the form of an imaginary view of the meandering course of the River Nile, with Alexandria and the Mediterranean coast in the foreground, and the temple of Isis on the island of Philae in the far distance. This pictorial view of Egypt, already incorporating the basic essentials of Egyptian architecture, from the pyramids at Giza to the temples of eastern and western Thebes, is a good metaphor for the speed with which the bare bones of Egyptology were assembled. As early as the 1830s, Gardner Wilkinson was able to present a wide-ranging and detailed view of ancient Egypt in his *Manners and Customs*. Certainly there were inaccuracies, misconceptions, and omissions in the publications of the early 19th century, but in many respects the fundamentals were already known, and the last one and a half centuries have arguably been more concerned with filling in the details than breaking new ground.

Between the period of organized plundering undertaken by such men as Giovanni Belzoni and Bernardino Drovetti in the early 19th century and the excavations of Émile Amélineau and Jacques de Morgan in the 1890s, there was surprisingly little development in the techniques employed by Egyptian archaeologists. John Wortham neatly encapsulates this phase in his history of British Egyptology: 'Although archaeologists no longer used dynamite to excavate sites, their techniques remained unrefined'.

Arguably one of the most insidious and retrogressive aspects of 19th-century archaeology in Egypt was the concept of 'clearance', as opposed to scientific excavation. The very word appeared to substantiate the fallacy that the sand simply had to be removed in order to reveal the significant monuments hidden below, thus helping to discourage the proper consideration of stratigraphic excavation and the appreciation of all components of a site—sand, potsherds, mud bricks, and towering stone gateways—as equally important and integral elements of the archaeological record. Such 'clearance' also frequently involved the destruction of the more recent material, primarily the Byzantine and Islamic phases of sites, which generally held little fascination for early scholars, compared with the pharaonic antiquities. From the 1880s onwards, however, the emergence of more scientific approaches gradually hauled Egyptology into a more methodical era.

In the late 19th and early 20th centuries, at a time when scientific methods of fieldwork and analysis were still developing throughout the various branches of archaeology, the innovative methods of two particular Egyptologists, Flinders Petrie and George Reisner, set new standards for the discipline as a whole. This was perhaps the only stage in its history when Egyptian archaeology was at the forefront of the development of methodology, setting the pattern for excavations in Europe and America.

In Bruce Trigger's *A History of Archaeological Thought*, there are a mere handful of references to Egyptian archaeology: only Flinders Petrie's invention of an early form of seriation known as 'sequence dating' merits a full page or so of discussion. While this may well be a fair assessment of the Egyptological contribution to archaeological *thought*, the excavation of Egyptian sites has, over the last 150 years, provided a steady stream of valuable *data*. The rapidly expanding Egyptian database has provided new insights into the material culture of the pharaonic period, but, perhaps more importantly, it has also made a significant contribution to the creation of a chronological framework for the Mediterranean region. The central role played by ancient Egypt in the formulation of ancient chronology has lent greater significance to recent attempts to pinpoint flaws in the chronology of the pharaonic period, but the established chronology is now a dense matrix of archaeological and textual details that have proved difficult to unpick and reassemble (see Chapter 3).

Chapter 2
Reconstructing ancient Egypt

The Narmer Palette was discovered about a metre away from a buried collection of ceremonial objects dating to the Late Predynastic and Early Dynastic periods (*c*.3100–2700 BC), including further ceremonial palettes, as well as ritual mace-heads and carved ivory figurines. This assemblage of artefacts discovered by Quibell and Green—and described by them as the 'main deposit'—has since proved to be one of the most important sets of evidence for our understanding of the beginnings of the Egyptian state. Unfortunately, because of a lack of accurate published plans and stratigraphic sections from the site, the full significance and the true date of this crucial early find remain unclear. In the vicinity, the excavators also discovered several valuable pieces from somewhat later in Egyptian history. These included two unique copper alloy statues of the late Old Kingdom ruler Pepi I (2321–2287 BC) and the golden head of a falcon that is perhaps part of one of the cult statues worshipped in the temple. The mixture of objects of different dates suggests that they comprised a whole series of royal gifts to the temple. However, we have no way of knowing whether each piece was brought to the temple in person by a number of rulers from the late Predynastic through to the Old Kingdom, or whether they were all dedicated en masse by a later ruler in the Old or Middle Kingdoms.

Some of Quibell's comments on the excavation of the 'main deposit' and the immediately surrounding area convey a rather honest despair that their techniques were not quite equal to the task:

> Day after day we sat in this hole, scraping away the earth, and trying to disentangle the objects from one another; for they lay in every possible position, each piece in contact with five or six others, interlocking as a handful of matches will, when shaken together and thrown down upon a table.

In *Egypt before the Pharaohs*, the American prehistorian Michael Hoffman summarized just how much of a hash seems to have been made by Quibell and Green (although it would also be a mistake to underestimate the complexity of their task at Hierakonpolis):

> Sadly we do not even know for sure where the most graphic piece of evidence, the Narmer Palette, actually came from. It was evidently found near the Main Deposit but not actually with the other material. From Green's field notes (Quibell kept none!) it seems to have been found a metre or two away, and Green noted in the 1902 publication that it was found in a place directly associated with an apparently Protodynastic level, which would date it to a generation or two before the unification of the Two Lands in 3100 B.C. But two years earlier, in the first report published on Hierakonpolis by Quibell, it was labelled as coming from the Main Deposit proper, a feature that may be as late as the Middle Kingdom (ca. 2130–1785 B.C.).

The particular nature and context of Quibell and Green's discovery of the Narmer Palette at Hierakonpolis highlight the fact that great finds can in extreme cases be rendered almost meaningless if their full context is not properly recorded. Even the most meticulous excavation may sometimes run up against interpretative problems, but, conversely, if discoveries are made or published in an unscientific way then there is only the slimmest chance of their full meaning becoming apparent. This is also true of the overall cultural contexts of late Predynastic ceremonial palettes like that of Narmer. David O'Connor, for instance, has raised the possibility that the images on the two sides of each palette were organized differently because they served distinct ritual functions within their practical religious settings, with the side that incorporated the cosmetic grinding area usually being uppermost and probably therefore more important. He also stresses, however, that the ceremonial palettes need to be seen as only tiny specific components within an overall complex of ritual images, objects, and architecture, only scattered fragments of which have survived from the late Predynastic and Early Dynastic periods.

Huge amounts of data have survived from ancient Egypt, and Egyptologists have consequently tended to be data-hungry scholars. A constant succession of fresh discoveries has ensured that the evidence itself has been steadily increasing in quantity and diversity. It is noticeable, however, that archaeological discoveries in Egypt have become such a cliché, in the way that the media respond to them and portray the discoveries and the protagonists, that an issue of *Punch* in 1986 was able to satirize very effectively the breathless and overblown way in which a new find (in this case the tomb of a man called Maya, Tutankhamun's treasurer) was pumped up into a mini-Tutankhamun's tomb.

The subject itself has not progressed purely through discoveries of new data. New paradigms have been adopted by different generations of Egyptologists, gradually transforming the accepted picture of ancient Egyptian culture. Secondly, new methods, such as innovative excavation techniques or sophisticated processes of scientific analysis, have, at various times, altered our perceptions of the surviving evidence from ancient Egypt. Whatever the hyperbole of the media, some of the archaeological discoveries have genuinely represented significant turning points in the history of the subject, as in the case of the excavation of Aegean-style frescos at the site of Tell el-Dab'a in 1987 or the unearthing of a rich cache of clay tablets inscribed in cuneiform script, at Amarna (the so-called Amarna Letters), in the 1890s. Like the Narmer Palette, both of these finds were quickly recognized not merely as crucial new pieces in the Egyptological jigsaw but as genuinely revolutionary types of information, necessitating significant rearrangement of the existing pattern of pieces.

The Avaris frescos

The Austrian Archaeological Institute (Cairo) has been excavating since the 1960s at Tell el-Dab'a, the site of the city of Avaris, capital of the Hyksos rulers from Syria–Palestine, who gained control of northern Egypt during the so-called Second Intermediate Period. The deep stratigraphy at Tell el-Dab'a allows the changing settlement patterns of a large Bronze Age community to be observed over a period of many generations. In the late 1980s the main focus of excavation was the substructure of a large palace building of the early 18th Dynasty (*c.*1550 BC) at Ezbet Helmi on the western edge of the site. In 1987 many fragments of Minoan wall-paintings were discovered among debris covering the ancient gardens adjoining the palace. Several of these derived from compositions evidently depicting 'bull-leapers', like those in the famous Middle Bronze Age palace at Knossos. Whereas the Minoan and Mycenaean pottery vessels previously found at many New Kingdom sites in Egypt are usually interpreted as evidence of trade with the Aegean, the presence of Minoan wall-paintings at Tell el-Dab'a hinted that the population of Avaris in the early 18th Dynasty may actually have included Aegean families. It has been suggested that the frequent use of a red painted background may even mean that the Avaris Minoan paintings pre-date those of Crete and Thera (Santorini).

The existence of Minoan wall-paintings at a site within Egypt may help to explain the appearance in early 18th-Dynasty Egyptian tomb paintings of such Aegean motifs as the 'flying gallop' (i.e. the depiction of animals' fore- and hindlegs outstretched in full flight). Were the Avaris paintings created by Minoan artists, or had Egyptian artists perhaps been trained by Minoans? Similar fragments of Minoan paintings have been found at three sites in the Levant (Tell Kabri, Qatna, and Alalakh), where they also appear to be associated with the ruling elite, as at Avaris. This discovery is one of a small number of crucial linchpins that are potentially able to link together the chronologies of various cultures across the East Mediterranean region.

The find also raises the question of what we mean by 'Minoan' culture. Until the discovery of the Avaris frescos, it was assumed that Crete was the source of this kind of 'Minoan' art, and that when it appeared elsewhere it was a sign of Cretan contact with other cultures in the Mediterranean, either through trade or population movement. The presence of 'Minoan' art in the Egyptian Delta, perhaps before it had appeared on Crete, suggests that it might have actually originated outside Crete, although the fact that this is so far the only recorded instance of this kind of art in Egypt probably makes it unlikely that Egyptian culture itself was the source.

The Amarna Letters

Like the Avaris frescos, the Amarna Letters were a 'non-Egyptian' find from within an Egyptian archaeological context. They are also similar in their far-reaching implications, since the Amarna Letters have come to exert a significant influence on our understanding of the politics and history of Egypt and the Near East in the late Bronze Age. The story of the Amarna Letters began in 1887 when a number of small clay tablets inscribed with the cuneiform script of Mesopotamia and the Levant were discovered by a village woman digging ancient mud brick for use as fertilizer (*sebakh* in Arabic). This discovery led to further illicit diggings and the appearance of a number of clay tablets on the antiquities market. Their importance was not immediately recognized, and many passed into private hands, but Wallis Budge of the British Museum believed the tablets to be genuine and purchased a number of them. It was Archibald Sayce, Professor of Assyriology at Oxford University at that time, who summed up their significance: 'A single archaeological discovery has upset mountains of learned discussion, of ingenious theory and sceptical demonstration.'

The subsequent excavations of Flinders Petrie at Amarna in 1891–2 revealed a few more tablets, thus confirming that the findspot of the bulk of the tablets was in the centre of the ancient city of Akhetaten, almost certainly from beneath the floor of a building identified by stamped mud bricks as 'Place of the Letters of Pharaoh', as well as nearby structures. Several further tablets were found by German and British excavators at Amarna in the first few decades of the 20th century, bringing the total to 382. These are now spread mainly between the collections of the British Museum, the Louvre, the Vorderasiatisches Museum in Berlin, and the Egyptian Museum in Cairo (although a few can also be found in other museums in Europe and the USA). Most of the finds came from the initial illicit digging at Amarna, rather than from scientific excavations, making the precise origins of over 90 per cent of the tablets uncertain. Their exact chronology is also still debated, but they span a 15–30-year period, beginning around year 30 of Amenhotep III (1391–1353) and extending no later than the first year of Tutankhamun's reign (1333–1323), with the majority dating to the reign of Akhenaten (1353–1335). Most are inscribed with texts in a dialect of the Akkadian language, which was the lingua franca of the time, although the languages of the Assyrians, Hittites, and Hurrians (Mitanni) are also represented.

The majority of the documents in the archive are items of diplomatic correspondence between Egypt and either the great powers in Western Asia, such as Babylonia and Assyria, or the vassal states of Syria and Palestine. They provide a fascinating picture of the relationships between Egypt and these states, although there are very few letters from the Egyptian rulers, the vast majority being the letters sent *to* them by other rulers. One interpretation of the letters is that they document the disintegration of the Egyptian Empire during the reign of Akhenaten, the so-called 'heretic pharaoh', who left few records of military campaigns and is therefore assumed to have neglected foreign policy in favour of a programme of religious and political reforms within Egypt itself. An alternative view would be that we happen by chance to have these documents from Akhenaten's reign, and that similar archives from earlier or later in the New Kingdom, had they survived, might contain equally desperate pleas for assistance from Syro-Palestinian cities under siege. In other words, it might be argued that our view of Egyptian influence over Syria–Palestine is largely based on the Egyptians' own accounts of their battles and victories, and that the chaotic state of affairs documented in the Amarna Letters might have actually been the normal condition of the Egyptian 'Empire' throughout the New Kingdom rather than being a temporary aberration.

Another controversy that has emerged out of the translation and interpretation of the Amarna Letters is the question of who the 'Apiru are. Many of the tablets from Syro-Palestinian vassals refer to a group of people called the 'Apiru, who appear to have been widespread across the Near East throughout the 2nd millennium BC. Since the first translations of the letters spelt the name Hapiru or Habiru, biblical scholars immediately began to explore the possibility that these were the first references to Hebrews, some even specifically correlating references to 'Apiru attacks with the account of Joshua's invasion of Canaan. However, there has not yet been any conclusive proof that the ethnic terms 'Apiru and Ibri (Hebrew) are linked etymologically, and it is not even clear whether 'Apiru refers to an ethnic group, a social group, or an economic class (or all three), with one commentator suggesting that the term was synonymous with 'social banditry'. As John Laughlin points out, 'it is certainly true to say that not all 'Apiru were Hebrews. Whether any Hebrews were ever 'Apiru is, at the moment, an open question.'

As well as giving insights into the political conditions of the time, the letters also shed light on trade relations and the values of particular commodities such as glass, gold, and the newly introduced iron, while the various forms of address employed in the letters indicate the standing of the writers vis-à-vis the Egyptian court. They have been used to study such issues as international law in the Amarna age, 'diplomatic signalling', and 'socio-psychological' analysis of Late Bronze Age diplomats and rulers.

Apart from this fresh textual scrutiny, the Amarna tablets have also been subjected to petrographic analysis to examine the actual clays from which they were formed, and compare them with the geology of various sites in the Mediterranean, the Near East, and North Africa in order to try to work out the places from which the letters were sent. Using this method, Dr Yuval Goren, an Israeli geologist, tackled the question of the whereabouts of the ancient kingdom of Alashiya, which was associated with the supply of copper to Egypt and other countries, and which might have been located in Cyprus, Cilicia, north-west Syria, or even southern Israel. The fabric of one of eight Alashiya letters in the British Museum looked quite different, suggesting that, unlike most of the tablets, it might not be an Egyptian-made local copy but might possibly be one of the original letters made from clay at Alashiya itself. It was made from a pinkish marly clay that includes many fragments of chlorite and dolerite, suggesting that the clay was obtained from a particular type of area dominated by igneous rock. Goren found that this helped to narrow down the likely choices to the Troodos massif on Cyprus, the region of Kizzuwatna in Anatolia, and the Biabashin region of north-west Syria. He was then able to rule out first Kizzuwatna, because it was governed by

Egypt's great rivals, the Hittites, and secondly the north-west Syrian area, because it seemed to be too geologically diverse to fit the bill. On Cyprus, on the other hand, there was one region that fitted the evidence in various ways. Geologically, the likely area was located between the doleritic Troodos mountains and the adjacent marly part of the island, which would have provided a pink clay with a mixture of dolerite and marly clay just like that of the tablet. Significantly, this area of Cyprus is also the area in which copper was being produced from the Middle Bronze Age onwards. Cyprus itself had always been the favourite candidate for the location of Alashiya, but Goren's analysis seems to provide good scientific support for the theory.

Although most of the Amarna archive consists of letters, it also includes thirty-two other kinds of texts that do not seem to have been directly connected with international diplomacy. These tablets were probably related to scribal education and the process of translation itself, including a dictionary-like list of Akkadian and Egyptian words, a fragment of a syllabary, as well as several scribal exercises and literary texts. We therefore not only have the royal correspondence itself, but also some of the evidence for the activities of the scribes employed to write and translate the letters.

Petrie's New Race, and other embarrassments

Our steadily adjusted and reframed picture of Egyptian civilization has periodically allowed earlier finds to be reviewed and reinterpreted, sometimes quite radically. Although the circumstances of the discovery of the Tell el-Dabʻa frescos and the Amarna Letters were quite different (and separated in date by around a century), both were nevertheless fairly rapidly recognized as important finds. There are, however, many instances of important finds that were at first totally misinterpreted or regarded as unremarkable, and only came to be recognized as really significant sources of evidence long after the discovery had been made.

One very good example of a great discovery that was initially completely misunderstood comes, surprisingly, from the career of the great Flinders Petrie. In his excavation of the Naqada cemeteries in 1895 he found that virtually all of the graves comprised rectangular, sometimes brick-lined, pits containing one or more bodies in foetal positions, placed on reed mats with the head oriented towards the west. Occasionally the bodies appeared to have been deliberately dismembered before burial, and there were some indications of human sacrifice. The varying quantities of grave goods usually consisted of some combination of pottery, stone vessels, greywacke palettes, flint knives, beads, bracelets, and figurines. Petrie immediately recognized that these were quite different from conventional Egyptian burials. However, his conclusion that they belonged to a 'New Race' from outside Egypt, who had supposedly invaded Egypt at the end of the Old Kingdom, was to turn out to be drastically wrong, both chronologically and ethnically. The most galling aspect of getting this wrong from Petrie's point of view was the fact that one of his great rivals, Jacques de Morgan, came up with the correct solution when he published a similar set of graves at Abydos. The people buried in the Naqada and Abydos cemeteries were different not because they were a 'New Race' but because they were the Egyptians of late prehistory whose long sequence of culture preceded the pharaonic period, and had until then been virtually unknown. As if to make amends for his colossal error, Petrie went on to use the Naqada material to develop the ingenious 'sequence dating' system, forming the basis for the first Predynastic chronology, which many would rate among his greatest achievements (Figure 4).

Conversely, some of the most famous finds made in Egypt have not necessarily had very significant effects on our views of Egypt. Howard Carter's discovery of the tomb of Tutankhamun, for instance, obviously had enormous impact on the public awareness of ancient Egypt from the 1920s onwards, but, apart from providing the first tantalizing glimpse of the sumptuous range of

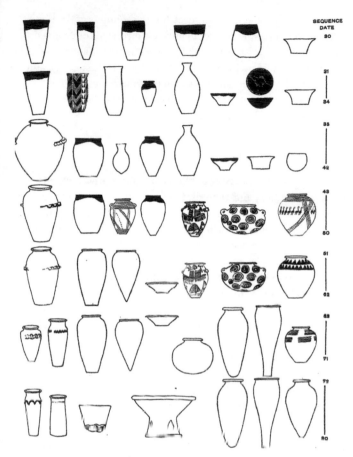

4. Part of Flinders Petrie's sequence dating system for pottery of the Predynastic period.

equipment which must once have been contained in the tombs of much more renowned and long-lived pharaohs, such as Amenhotep III and Ramesses the Great, it contributed very little genuinely new historical data. Arguably Carter's greatest achievement was to raise the public profile of Egyptian archaeology to a much higher level, but the contents of the tomb have not yet taken the subject in any new directions or changed opinions on any great historical debates. The tomb is of course arguably the most exciting find in the history of archaeology, and its contents have increasingly yielded information on various aspects of the technology of the 14th century BC—but Egyptologists can be very difficult to please . . .

Egyptology embracing science

As a result of the increasing application of innovative methods of survey, excavation, and analysis, the professional archaeologist has begun to require at least a nodding acquaintance with a number of scientific disciplines, such as bioanthropology, geology, genetics, and physics. This process of expansion of Egyptology has added strength to the subject, with each of these different academic disciplines providing fresh sources of stimulation and new directions for future research.

In Carter's time, science was only just beginning to have an effect on the world of Egyptology, primarily in the form of a man called Alfred Lucas, who, within four years of the discovery of Tutankhamun's tomb, was to publish the first edition of *Ancient Egyptian Materials and Industries*, a brilliant summary of the surviving evidence for Egyptian materials and craftwork, which served as the essential manual for Egyptological science until the 1990s. Lucas was a chemist working in Cairo, who had access to much of the material in the Egyptian museum, enabling him to publish data, chemical analyses, and bibliographical references for a great deal of the most important material excavated since the mid-19th century, including the objects from the tomb of Tutankhamun.

There are two aspects of the study of ancient Egypt that have been repeatedly affected by science over the last fifty years. First, the use of science has meant that some elements of the archaeological record that were previously regarded as relatively uninformative, such as soil and seeds, have begun to produce as much information as more traditional finds, such as sculptures and papyri. Second, the application of scientific techniques has allowed more information to be squeezed out of conventional types of evidence. Mummified bodies, instead of simply being unwrapped and examined externally, can now be X-rayed and CT-scanned in various ways, and DNA samples can reveal a great deal more about the nature and identity of the specific human or animal concerned. Artefacts can be studied not only in terms of their shape, size, and decoration but also with regard to the type of material from which they were made: where it came from, how it was extracted, and what techniques were used to transform it into a prestige funerary item. Indeed, the whole question of the procurement and working of materials has become a much more frequently researched aspect of ancient Egypt over the last two decades or so.

What can geology and archaeology tell us about the origins of the Narmer Palette?

The Narmer Palette was carved from a type of rock geologically known as greywacke (but often mistakenly described as schist or slate), which was used for a variety of artefacts in the Predynastic period. By Early Dynastic times, this versatile material was even being used for sculpture, including a seated statue of the 2nd-Dynasty ruler Khasekhemwy, which was found near the Narmer Palette at Hierakonpolis, and is now in the Egyptian Museum, Cairo.

The only good-quality source of ancient Egyptian greywacke is located in the Wadi Hammamat, in the centre of the Eastern Desert, midway between the Nile Valley city of Quft and the Red Sea port of Quseir. The quarries were worked for thousands of years, from the Predynastic period through to Roman times (c.4000 BC–AD 500). Hundreds of rock-cut inscriptions and numerous quarry workings are spread along a 16 km stretch of the wadi, west of the confluence with Wadi Atolla. The site has been studied by many archaeologists and Egyptologists over the last century, but most have tended to focus on the inscriptions rather than the archaeological remains or the rock art. A huge Roman-period quarriers' ramp runs up the south side of the wadi, while on the floor of the wadi on the north side are the ruins of a small area of settlement that so far seems to date no earlier than the mid-1st millennium BC.

The current geoarchaeological expedition working at the site, led by Dr Elizabeth Bloxam, not only chooses to focus much more on the archaeology of all periods at the site but also takes a pioneering holistic approach to the Wadi Hammamat as a whole, allowing the textual sources and archaeological material to be studied contextually in their full range of spatial and chronological relationships with one another. Throughout the pharaonic period, the greywacke quarries were exploited for large objects such as sarcophagi, naoi, and sculptures (Figure 5), but there was an important much earlier phase of exploitation, from at least the 4th millennium BC onwards, when the stone was used to produce smaller artefacts, particularly beads, bracelets, vessels, and ritual cosmetic palettes, including, of course, the Narmer Palette itself.

The earliest period of quarrying at the site had not previously been studied, apart from a small amount of survey and excavation conducted in 1949 by the prehistorian Fernand Debono. His pioneering survey of the Egyptian Eastern Desert included study of a number of Predynastic burials and settlements sporadically spaced along the 150 km stretch of the Wadi Hammamat, but this work was only partially published. In 2010, Bloxam's team decided to seek out the Predynastic and Early Dynastic quarries, and the workshops associated with them. The one clue they had initially was a photograph that Debono had taken showing an early workshop and settlement that he had excavated in the Bir Hammamat region. The location of the photograph was extremely

5. Greywacke triad of the 4th-Dynasty ruler Menkaura, flanked by the goddess Hathor (left) and a personification of the jackal province (right), *c.*2460 BC (Cairo, Egyptian Museum).

difficult to identify, until they chanced on a rock-carved graffito left by Debono himself, which then allowed them to identify the workshop, on a gravelly terrace just yards away. Subsequently they found a smaller, but better preserved, workshop, also on a slightly elevated area at the edge of the wadi, where both bracelets and palettes were being manufactured, with several fragments of pottery dating the activities to the mid to late Predynastic period (*c*.3500–3000 BC). They found several discs of greywacke partially worked into bracelets, as well as two palette rough-outs, and it was clear that a range of tools were being used to produce finished items in the workshops. Chert bladelets and crescent drills, as well as silicified sandstone borers and grinders, were among a suite of largely imported specialist stone tools used by the crafts people. These tools, whether imported as raw materials or already fashioned into toolkits, can only have been brought into the workshops by people arriving from elsewhere, given that chert and silicified sandstone deposits of such quality are not local to the site. This fresh evidence has provided intriguing insights into the extent of specialist local and regional craft mobility during the Predynastic.

Debono, however, had not located any of the early quarries supplying the workshops—where were they? As Bloxam and her team conducted their survey of the quarrying region, they discovered one useful practical thing. If you want to move rapidly around the Hammamat landscape you need to get up onto the mountains and ridges adjoining the main wadi, rather than trudging through endless smaller wadis where progress is slow, visibility of the surrounding area is poor, and it is very easy to get lost, even when only a hundred yards or so off the beaten track. The team therefore followed a hunch that the earliest quarriers might have had the same kind of mobility issues, leading them to site their quarries up in the hills overlooking the main wadi, where they could be accessed without descending to the main wadi floor. Eventually the team found the first of numerous small quarries high above the wadi, where rough-outs for palettes, vessels, and bracelets clearly indicated that greywacke was being hacked out of the mountainside for these Predynastic and Early Dynastic artefacts. The early quarries typically took the form of platforms carved out of the steep mountain slope, creating a narrow terrace no more than 30 metres in length and therefore probably only able to accommodate groups of up to ten workers at any one time. The quarries were interconnected by numerous heavily worn mountain paths, mostly still clearly visible even after the passage of thousands of years, suggesting frequent movement of quarriers and craftsmen across the highland landscape. It was noticeable that panels of rock art often seemed to be located at the entrances to subsidiary quarries leading up to these higher places, as if acting as signposts.

Bloxam knew from the comparative archaeology of quarries many thousands of miles away—such as the Neolithic greenstone quarries in the English Lake District and the Mount William Aboriginal stone axe quarries in Australia—that choices made by ancient quarriers could often have as much to do with issues relating to ritual, landscape, and social interconnections as with purely geological or logistical factors. As she puts it: 'we cannot discard the numerous cross-cultural examples in which rock art and quarrying are linked together, typically as a nexus between people, marking a symbolic, even spiritual connection with places to which individuals and groups frequently returned.' She stresses the likelihood that the early quarry-workers—one of whom would have skilfully roughed out the basic shield shape of the Narmer Palette on one of these precipitous terraces high above the main Wadi Hammamat—were probably local kin-groups made up of specialists, extracting and shaping the rock with pounders, axes, and chisels (fashioned both from the local greywacke itself and from non-local types of flint and silicified sandstone). Ironically, it seems that the origins of the Narmer Palette lay far from the Nile Valley itself, in the hands of workers, perhaps Bedouin, who might not even have identified as ancient Egyptians themselves.

Chapter 3
History

One of the fundamental questions often asked about the Narmer Palette is whether, as its discoverers assumed, it was created as a record of a specific historical event: the military triumph on which the first unified kingdom of Upper and Lower Egypt was founded. The palette and various other 'protodynastic' artefacts have long been regarded as lying at the interface of prehistory and history in ancient Egypt. The term protodynastic was invented to describe the crucial period encompassing the late Predynastic and the beginning of the Early Dynastic period. The 'Predynastic' was the last few hundred years of the long prehistoric period in the Nile Valley, while 'Early Dynastic' refers to the first few centuries of the dynastic or pharaonic period (see timeline at the back of the book).

At the time of the discovery of the Narmer Palette, the Predynastic period was barely known at all, since it was not until the following year that Flinders Petrie published the first chronological framework for late prehistory, using 'sequence dates' based on changing fashions of artefacts in grave goods at the Predynastic Naqada cemeteries (Figure 4). This means that the chronological context of the palette would have been seen quite differently by Quibell and Green compared with modern researchers. Whereas most Egyptologists now see this crucial artefact as part of the culmination of a long period of late Predynastic cultural development, including a developing corpus of decorated palettes, its discoverers regarded it as the first real 'document' in recorded history, emerging almost magically out of what seemed then to be the darkness of prehistory. The palette immediately began to be interpreted as a record of the first truly significant historical 'event' in Egyptian history: the military defeat of Lower Egypt (the Delta region in the north) by the ruler of an expanding Upper Egyptian kingdom.

When the British Egyptologist Bryan Emery made the first real attempt to summarize the nature of Early Dynastic Egypt with the publication of *Archaic Egypt* in 1961, a great deal of the primary evidence was freshly excavated, much of it by himself and his contemporaries or immediate predecessors. There was also, of course, a large quantity of evidence that had not yet been excavated, particularly with regard to the thousands of years preceding the emergence of the early Egyptian state. When Emery was writing, Egyptian prehistory, like many other aspects of the modern discipline, was still very much in its infancy, so it is not surprising to find that he constantly looks forwards into the pharaonic period for comparisons and analogies that can anchor his subject as a specific stage of the Egyptians' cultural development. In contrast, recent books and articles on Early Dynastic Egypt tend to be more firmly rooted in the late Predynastic. Indeed, the fresh excavation of early cemeteries at Abydos in the last two decades of the 20th century provided new evidence for the existence of a politically and/or culturally united Egypt well before the 1st Dynasty. Work in the late Predynastic 'Cemetery U' at Abydos, comprising elite tombs dating earlier than the time of King Narmer, demonstrated that certain elements of Egyptian kingship (including a model royal sceptre, carved from ivory) stretched back at least 150 years earlier than the beginning of the 1st Dynasty.

Many modern Egyptologists have applied explicitly anthropological approaches to the study of the formation of the state in early complex societies, but for Emery's generation of archaeologists, the 'culture history' approach was still the main paradigm in archaeology. In the first half of the 20th century, most archaeologists thought that cultural change happened primarily because of the diffusion of either people or ideas between cultural or ethnic groups. Thus the prehistoric development of Egypt tended to be explained in terms of mass migrations.

Emery was keen to promote the idea that the emergence of Egyptian civilization at the end of the 4th millennium was the result of the invasion or immigration of the so-called Dynastic Race (or 'Followers of Horus') from Mesopotamia. Now, however, the massive advances in our knowledge of prehistory and recent excavations of Predynastic and early Dynastic sites, particularly the early royal necropolis at Abydos and the city and cemetery at Hierakonpolis, have demonstrated extremely convincingly that the development and inauguration of the pharaonic age was largely an indigenous Egyptian phenomenon, arising steadily, and almost inevitably, out of processes of late Predynastic social, economic, and political change within the Nile Valley.

Interpreting early palettes and mace-heads— extracting myth and history

From the Palaeolithic period onwards, people in Egypt were using flat pieces of stone as palettes on which to grind mineral-based pigments such as ochre and malachite. Initially they were simple slabs made from a variety of different stone types, but from the early Predynastic period (*c.*4500–4000 BC) onwards they were made largely of greywacke quarried from the Wadi Hammamat (as discussed at the end of Chapter 2). It was also in the early Predynastic that people began to fashion the palettes into distinctive shapes (initially long oval forms, with a notch at each end), often placing them in graves as part of the funerary equipment, sometimes accompanied by red or brown jasper

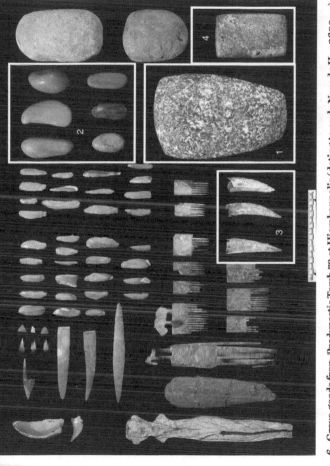

6. Grave-goods from Predynastic Tomb 72 at Hierakonpolis (dating to early Naqada II, *c*.3600 BC), including two diorite palettes (1 & 4), pebbles for grinding pigments (2), and the tusk tips used to hold ochre pigment (3); the tomb also contained a very unusual early male figurine carved in ivory, shown bottom-left here.

pebbles that were probably used for grinding. In 2013, two diorite palettes stained with malachite and ochre were excavated from Tomb 72, in the Predynastic cemetery HK6 at Hierakonpolis, which is an unusual and highly elaborate elite burial dating to *c.*3700–3600 BC (Figure 6). In this instance, the palettes were accompanied not only by pebbles but also by a unique find of three tips of ivory tusks used as containers for yellow ochre.

It is unclear whether the pigments ground on the Predynastic palettes were used for production of paints and dyes decorating such things as pottery vessels and early textiles, or whether they were primarily used for cosmetics, such as eye-paint. Evidence for use of cosmetics at this date includes a terracotta figurine from a grave at Mahasna dating to Naqada I (*c.*3800–3600 BC) which seems to have its eyes outlined in green, while traces of malachite have been found on naturally mummified individuals excavated from the Predynastic cemetery at Adaima.

Predynastic palettes were fashioned into a wide variety of shapes, which changed over time, from the oval Badarian palettes, through to predominantly rhomboidal ones in the Naqada I period (occasionally with small motifs, such as bird-shapes, sculpted at one end) and animal, fish, and bird forms in Naqada II (*c.*3600–3350 BC) (Figure 7). Interestingly, these zoomorphic themes are mirrored in the shapes of other objects placed in graves at this time, such as stone vessels and bone and ivory combs. In Naqada III (*c.*3350–3000 BC), the final phase of the Predynastic period, there was a return to more geometric forms, particularly simple rectangles. The surfaces of some of these later palettes are sculpted with images of various types. A palette from a grave at el-Amra (British Museum 35501), for example, is carved with a combination of two early hieroglyphs (a sign comprising oppositely facing arrow heads superimposed over another representing a crook or staff), usually interpreted as the symbol representing the god Min. These relatively simple decorated palettes can perhaps be seen as earlier prototypes of the larger,

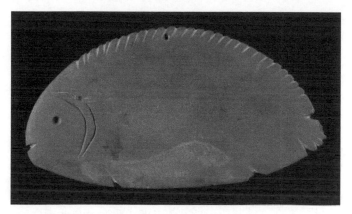

7. Predynastic greywacke palette in the shape of a fish, dating to the Naqada I period, *c*.3800–3500 BC (British Museum EA57947).

more ceremonial palettes exemplified by that of Narmer. The ceremonial palettes, which began to appear in the Naqada III period, tend to be primarily associated with temple contexts rather than tombs. More than twenty-five of them have so far been found, and their decoration is more closely associated with that of ceremonial mace-heads and ivory knife-handles than with the funerary palettes.

Several significant votive palettes and mace-heads were found by Quibell and Green at Hierakonpolis, including limestone fragments from a large, pear-shaped mace-head that, like the Narmer Palette, bears early hieroglyphic signs spelling out the name Narmer. This 'Narmer Mace-head' appears to show not warlike scenes but ones that are more obviously to do with early rituals associated with kingship, one of which is regarded by some researchers as the first known version of the ritual known as *ḫ'ty-bity*: 'the appearance of the King of Lower Egypt'. Fragments were also found of another limestone mace-head (now in the Ashmolean Museum, Oxford) also decorated with raised relief scenes, including a man wearing the Upper Egyptian White

Crown. This individual is the largest figure on the mace-head, and an accompanying ideogram appears to identify him as King Scorpion, who might have been Narmer's predecessor on the throne. The figure of Scorpion is grasping a large hoe, while a servant holds out to him a basket, perhaps in order to catch the earth that he is removing from the ground. The fact that he and his servant are standing immediately beside some kind of water-course has led to suggestions that he is ritually excavating an irrigation canal with the help of attendants. As a result of this interpretation, which is widely held but not necessarily conclusively proven, the Scorpion Mace-head has frequently been used as a crucial piece of evidence in the hypothesis that the Egyptian state, and its characteristic monarchical style of government, emerged through the control of water by an elite group.

The Canadian Egyptologist Nick Millet argued that the images and texts on the ceremonial palettes and mace-heads of the late 4th and early 3rd millennia were not intended to describe historical events in themselves but simply to commemorate and date particular points in time. He suggested that the scenes on the Narmer Mace-head resemble the brief lists of rituals given for each year of a series of early kings' reigns on the Palermo Stone (part of a large 5th-Dynasty basalt stele recording the reigns of several early Egyptian rulers, which is discussed in more detail in the section on chronologies below).

Our analysis of the scenes and texts on objects such as the Narmer Palette and Mace-head is generally complicated by the modern urge to be able to distinguish between 'real' events and rituals. But the ancient Egyptians show very little inclination to distinguish consistently between the two, and indeed it might be argued that Egyptian ideology during the pharaonic period—particularly insofar as it related to the kingship—was reliant on the maintenance of some degree of confusion between real happenings and purely ritual or magical acts. The texts and artefacts that form the basis of Egyptian history usually convey information which is either general (mythological or ritualistic) or particular (historical), and usually our aim in constructing Egyptian historical narrative is to distinguish as clearly as possible between these types of information, taking into account the ancient Egyptians' tendency to blur the boundaries between the two.

This debate concerning rituals, symbols, and historical events was given an intriguing new twist in the late 1990s, when a German excavation team re-examined the early royal burials at Abydos. In tomb B16, they found an almost complete ivory label decorated with images closely resembling some of those on the Narmer Palette (Figure 8). Like most other surviving examples of this kind of label found both in the Early Dynastic royal tombs and the late Predynastic elite burials of Cemetery U, it was made in order to identify the quality, quantity, and year of delivery of a product (usually a vessel containing imported oil) placed in the tomb. A small hole bored in the top right-hand corner was intended to attach it to the vessel, and the lower of two lines of incised hieroglyphic inscription identified it as '300 units of first-quality oil'.

It is the upper line of inscription on the Narmer label that is the most relevant to our discussion, however, since it closely resembles the smiting scene on the Narmer Palette, except that in this instance the image is transformed into a form of hieroglyphic sentence comprising the name Narmer, which appears twice, once on the right-hand side in a *serekh* frame (as on the palette) and once in the middle of the inscription but this time with two arms having been added to the *nar* hieroglyph (the catfish sign) so that it can wield a mace with one hand and grasp a bearded foreigner with the other. The foreigner sprouts plants from his head (like the schematic man held prisoner by the Horus falcon on the palette) and has a small 'bowl' hieroglyph to his left. At the top left a vulture hovers over a rectangle perhaps representing the royal

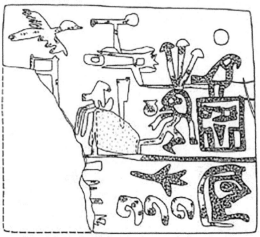

8. Ivory label (probably originally attached to an oil vessel) from tomb B16 at Abydos, bearing an animated version of the name of King Narmer, in which a catfish strikes a foreigner with a mace, *c.*3000 BC (Cairo, Egyptian Museum).

palace, with a falcon-topped standard in front of it. This is very plausibly interpreted as the sentence 'Smiting the Libyan marshland people by Horus Narmer, celebration (of victory) of the palace'. Since it presumably identifies a specific year in the king's reign, as the other labels do, it seems likely that it identifies the same year as the scenes depicted on the Narmer Palette. In addition, a tiny ivory cylinder bearing the name of Narmer was found at Hierakonpolis and probably also belongs to the same year in his reign, since it shows the catfish smiting three rows of foreign captives identified with the same word *tjehenw* (usually translated as Libyans).

Taken together, the label, the cylinder, and the palette seem to confirm Millet's idea that the labels and the votive items are all decorated with information describing a particular year in a king's reign. The excavator of the label, German Egyptologist Günter Dreyer, argued that this combination of evidence proved that Narmer's defeat of northerners/Libyans was an actual historical event. This assessment, however, seems rather premature. An alternative assumption would be that we simply now have three records of the same event, but we are no closer to knowing whether it was a genuine historical military victory, purely a kingship ritual with no basis in reality, or perhaps even a ceremonial re-enactment of some actual earlier triumph.

What is Egyptian history?

Historians of ancient Egypt sometimes attempt to interpret the Egyptian sources with modern concepts and categories that would have had no real meaning or relevance to the ancient writers. The types of ancient Egyptian texts that are usually described as 'historical' invariably had a very different function when they were originally composed; they therefore have to be carefully interpreted if genuinely historical data are to be extracted from them. The vast majority of alleged historical texts written by the Egyptians were primarily concerned with preserving and transmitting national traditions or with fulfilling a particular religious or funerary role, rather than being attempts to present objective accounts of the past. The ancient Egyptians' own presentations of their past might be regarded as 'celebrations' of both continuity and change.

Even the Egyptian royal narratives, such as the two stelae of Kamose (*c.*1555–1550) describing his battles against the Hyksos in the 17th Dynasty, and the annals of Thutmose III (*c.*1479–1425), outlining his campaigns in Syria–Palestine in the 18th Dynasty, are effectively components of the temples in which they were found, therefore they differ considerably from the true historical tradition usually said to have been inaugurated by the Greek historian Herodotus, in that they incorporate a high degree of symbolism and pure ritual. The contents of the monumental texts and reliefs on the walls of Egyptian tombs and temples are often much more related to the symbolic and static world of myth than to history. There is a common tendency to regard myth as a form of 'primitive history', but this is rarely the case. Donald Redford makes a good distinction between Egyptian myth and history:

> Their meaning [i.e. the meaning of myths] has nothing to do with their having occurred in the past, but rather with their present significance . . . Horus's championing of his father, the upliftings of Shu, the murder of Osiris—these are all primordial events, timeless and ever-present; and neither king nor priest who re-enacts them can be said to fulfil an historic role, or to be commemorating 'history'.

What is the basis for Egyptian chronology?

Without some form of chronological framework, history is nothing but an unstructured mass of data. There are numerous ways in which Egyptologists have set about creating such a framework for ancient Egypt, using a complex mixture of archaeological data (such as coffins bearing different types of decoration), texts (such as 'annals' and 'king-lists'), ancient astronomical observations, and scientific dating methods (such as radiocarbon dating and, much more rarely, thermoluminescence).

Egyptologists use the term 'royal annals' to describe a number of ancient Egyptian texts that either list the names and titles of a sequence of rulers (often called 'king-lists'), or present information about events that took place in specific reigns and even individual years within reigns. Virtually all of the surviving examples derive from religious or funerary contexts and many—particularly the simple lists of names and titles—relate to the celebration of the cult of royal ancestors, whereby each king established his own legitimacy and place in the succession by making regular offerings to a list of the names of his predecessors. The annals have survived in various forms, mostly dating to the New Kingdom, but the earliest is the so-called Palermo Stone, a large fragment of a basalt stele in the Palermo Archaeological Museum, Sicily, which dates to the 5th Dynasty (*c.*2494–2345).

The Palermo Stone is inscribed on both sides with hieroglyphic texts describing the reigns of the kings of the first five dynasties, as well as the preceding era of mythological rulers. The size of the original complete stele is estimated to have been about 2.1 m wide by 0.6 m high, and six smaller fragments of it have also survived (five in the Egyptian Museum, Cairo, and one in the Petrie Museum, University College London). The seven fragments mostly feature 1st and 4th Dynasty rulers. We have no information about the stele's original findspot, since the main fragment appeared on the antiquities market in 1866, but without provenance. The text begins with many thousands of years taken up by mythological Upper and Lower Egyptian Predynastic rulers up to the time of the god Horus who is then said to have given the throne to Menes, generally regarded by ancient Egyptians as the first human ruler of the pharaonic period. The complete stele originally listed Menes' successors up to the early 5th Dynasty. The text is divided into a series of horizontal registers split up by vertical lines, incurved at the top, to represent the hieroglyph for regnal year (*renpet*). Each compartment incorporated a brief list of memorable events for that year, as well a record of the height of the annual Nile inundation. The events recorded were mostly religious festivals, wars, and the creation of particular statues: they therefore actually tell us less about history and more about the early royal court and the emergence of the idea of divine kingship. The name of the ruler concerned is written above the relevant block of compartments. It is frustrating to know that a record detailing every ruler up until the end of Dynasty 5, along with the lengths of their reigns, once existed but that only fragments of it are now within our grasp. A similar Old Kingdom set of annals, known as the South Saqqara Stone, was found in the 1930s, having been recycled as the sarcophagus lid of Ankhesenpepi, one of the queens at this date. The text of the South Saqqara Stone, listing events in the reigns of several 6th-Dynasty rulers, was probably inscribed in the reign of Pepi II, but the signs had mostly been erased through the reuse of the slab.

Another tantalizing surviving fragment is the 'Mitrahina day-book', originally an Old Kingdom relief block that was inscribed, centuries later, with the earliest known example of Middle Kingdom royal annals. This section of annals, describing parts of two years in the reign of the 12th-Dynasty pharaoh Amenemhat II, was itself later reused as part of the western gateway of the New Kingdom temple of Ptah, near the modern village of Mitrahina, which occupies part of the site of the ancient capital city of Memphis. Unlike the Palermo Stone and South Saqqara Stone, both of which primarily summarize ritual events for each year of the various kings' reigns, the Mitrahina inscription provides quite detailed information, including brief reports of military campaigns and trading expeditions.

There are, in addition, several monumental 'king-lists' from religious and funerary contexts, each consisting of a simple list of rulers, and all compiled in the New Kingdom. Two were carved into walls at the Abydos temples of Seti I and Ramesses II respectively (the former still *in situ* and the latter in the British Museum), and another was carved in Karnak temple during the reign of Thutmose III (now in the Louvre). Several other king-lists decorated tomb walls, including two lists of 4th- and 5th-Dynasty kings in early 5th-Dynasty *mastaba*-tombs at Giza; the so-called Saqqara Tablet (now in the Egyptian Museum, Cairo), which derives from the tomb of Thuneroy, a high official of Ramesses II; and a scene in the tomb of an 18th-Dynasty priest called Amenmes at Thebes (TT373, *c.*1300 BC), showing the deceased venerating the statues of thirteen previous rulers.

Only one example of this 'king-list' genre was written on papyrus in the hieratic script, and therefore arguably archival rather than ceremonial in nature—this was the Turin Papyrus (also known as the Turin Royal Canon); like two of the stone-cut hieroglyphic examples, it dates to the reign of Ramesses II. The text not only lists a long sequence of rulers but also gives the precise duration of each reign, and occasionally provides a summary of the number of years that had elapsed since the time of Menes. In 1820 this papyrus was purchased in Luxor by the Italian diplomat and antiquities collector Bernardino Drovetti, and is now in the Museo Egizio, Turin. At the time that it was acquired by Drovetti, it was evidently still almost complete, but it suffered badly before entering the Turin collection, and is now highly fragmentary.

Over the last two centuries, the work of various Egyptologists, from Jean-François Champollion through to Jaromir Malek and Kim Ryholt, led to the numerous fragments of the Turin Canon being placed in the correct order, although many lacunae still remain. Originally it must have contained around 300 names, even including the Asiatic 'Hyksos' rulers of the Second Intermediate Period (although with a sign to indicate that they were foreigners, and no royal cartouche shape around the names), and ending with Ramesses II. Like the Palermo Stone, the list attempted to go back beyond the reigns of known kings and to

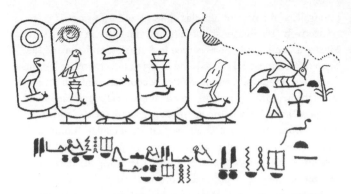

9. Wadi Hammamat King-list: rock inscription, dated to the Middle Kingdom on palaeographic grounds, found at Wadi el-Fawakhir in the Wadi Hammamat. It consists of five royal names and a short honorary prayer; the five names are (right to left): Khufu, Radjedef, Khafra, Hordjedefra, and Baufra.

assign reign lengths to the unnamed spirits and gods who had supposedly ruled before the coming of the first pharaoh.

There are also a few much briefer king-lists in a variety of contexts and media, such as a rock-cut graffito at the quarrying site of Wadi Hammamat, dated palaeographically to the 12th Dynasty (1991–1783), which consists of the names of five 4th-Dynasty rulers and princes (Figure 9). Two Early Dynastic seal impressions were discovered by German archaeologists in tombs Q and T at Abydos in the 1985 and 1995 excavations respectively. They were carved with short sequences of 1st-Dynasty rulers' names, one of them listing six rulers in the following order: Narmer, Aha, Djer, Djet, Den, and Merneith, thus providing another crucial piece of evidence that the king depicted on the Narmer Palette was probably the earliest in the sequence of 1st-Dynasty rulers. The so-called Giza King-list is a wooden, gypsum-coated writing board, which was found in a pit beside the Old Kingdom *mastaba*-tomb G1011, and is now in the Boston Museum of Fine

Arts. It is inscribed with the names of six Old Kingdom rulers from different dynasties.

Finally, the most detailed historical source is the *Aegyptiaca*, a history of Egyptian rulers compiled by a Hellenicized Egyptian priest called Manetho in early Ptolemaic times (3rd century BC). This has unfortunately survived only in the form of extracts quoted by much later historians from Josephus (1st century AD) to George Syncellus (early 9th century AD). Manetho was evidently able to consult both Egyptian sources, such as the royal annals described above, and also Greek historical texts. He probably wrote his history (dedicated to Ptolemy II) during the time that he was employed at the temple of Sebennytos, near the modern town of Samannud in the Delta. His division of the sequence of earthly (i.e. post-mythological) rulers into 30 dynasties (to which a 31st, the 2nd Persian Period, was later added) has been a major influence on the conventional view of Egyptian chronology since the early 19th century.

However, as the sources of Egyptian historical and archaeological data have inexorably expanded and diversified, with translations of new texts and excavations of fresh sites, it has become apparent that Manetho's chronological system is fatally flawed in one respect—it makes the basic assumption that there was one long sequence of Egyptian rulers governing the entire country, without overlaps between reigns and without fragmentation into mini-kingdoms. Over the years, research has increasingly demonstrated that Egypt was, at various times, not culturally unified and politically centralized, with changes taking place at different speeds in the various regions. Other analyses show that short-term political events, which have tended to be regarded as the paramount factors in history, may often have been less historically significant than the gradual socio-economic processes that can change the cultural landscape more overwhelmingly in the long term.

There are in fact several major problems with the traditional chronology. First, Manetho's history is frequently unreliable because we only have surviving quoted fragments rather than the whole original text, and because we do not know his sources. Second, there is often uncertainty regarding the lengths of kings' reigns: for instance, the Turin Canon says that Senusret II and III have reigns of 19 and 39 years respectively, whereas their highest recorded regnal years on actual monuments are 6 and 19. Third, there has been a major problem with the so-called 'intermediate periods', which were once lazily interpreted as rather impenetrable 'dark ages', but have gradually begun to be appreciated as complex and important chronological entities. Fourthly, there is still considerable controversy concerning overlaps between succeeding reigns (known as coregencies), especially in the 6th and 18th Dynasties. Finally, much of the traditional chronology hinges on ancient Egyptian documents that record astronomical observations, particularly of the 'heliacal rising' of the dog-star Sirius (i.e. the first morning in each year when this star became visible on the horizon, just before sunrise).

It began to be realized in the 1980s that the very small number of surviving texts that mention the heliacal rising of Sirius could provide different absolute dates depending on where the ancient astronomer-priests made their observations. Some Egyptologists, such as Rolf Krauss, have suggested that all the sightings were made at one place, and that this place might usually have been Elephantine, which was not only the southernmost Egyptian city (whose inhabitants would therefore have been the first to see the heliacal rising each year) but also the place most closely associated with measurement of the height of the annual inundation, which normally coincided with the heliacal rising of Sirius. Other scholars, such as William Ward, have argued that they must have all been local observations, i.e. the religious festivals timed to coincide with astronomical events might actually have taken place on different days in different parts of the country. A papyrus from

Lahun (Berlin 10012) dates a record of the heliacal rising of Sirius to the seventh year of the reign of Senusret III, which is often assumed to convert into an 'absolute' date of 1872 BC. However, if the observation was made in Elephantine, the absolute date could have been as late as 1830 BC, whereas if it was made in the northern city of Memphis, it could have been as early as 1880 BC. The difference between these two dates is significant—it is, for instance, considerably longer than the average ancient Egyptian's life-span in the 19th century BC, which is estimated to have been around 35 years even for elite men (and 30 for elite women, the latter dying earlier on average because of the perils of ancient childbirth).

Even the significance of the most basic historical divisions (i.e. the distinctions between the Predynastic, pharaonic, Ptolemaic, and Roman periods) has begun to be questioned. On the one hand, the results of excavations during the 1980s and 1990s in the cemeteries of Umm el-Qa'ab at Abydos suggest that before the 1st Dynasty there was also a Dynasty 0 stretching back for some unknown period into the 4th millennium. This means that, at the very least, the last one or two centuries of the 'Predynastic' were probably in many respects politically and socially 'Dynastic'.

Conversely, the increasing realization that late Predynastic pottery types were still widely used in the Early Dynastic period shows that certain cultural aspects of the Predynastic period continued on into the pharaonic period. The long 'pre-Dynastic' periods of Egyptian prehistory are inevitably understood as sequences of cultural rather than political developments. Now the Dynastic period (as well as the Ptolemaic and Roman periods) has begun to be understood not only as a traditional sequence of individual kings and ruling families but also as a cultural continuum, in which there were gradual changes in such factors as the types of clay being used for pottery and the styles and materials of many other types of artefact.

Whereas there are definite political breaks between the pharaonic and Ptolemaic periods, and between the Ptolemaic and Roman periods, the gradually increasing archaeological data from the two latter periods has begun to create a situation where the process of cultural change may be seen to be less sudden than the purely political records suggest. It is apparent, for instance, that many aspects of the ideology and material culture of the Ptolemaic period remain virtually unaltered by political upheavals. Instead of the arrival of Alexander the Great and his general Ptolemy representing a great watershed in Egyptian history, it might well be argued that, although there were certainly a number of significant *political* changes between the mid-1st millennium BC and the mid-1st millennium AD, these took place amid comparatively leisurely processes of social and economic change. Significant elements of pharaonic civilization survived relatively intact for several millennia, only undergoing a full combination of both cultural and political transformation at the beginning of the Islamic period in AD 641.

Radiocarbon dating and its changing roles in Egyptian chronology

A piece of wood from the Step Pyramid complex of the 3rd-Dynasty ruler Djoser was central to the first proof of the effectiveness of radiocarbon dating in 1949, when Willard Libby and James Arnold published their analyses of several samples of material from Egypt and Turkey. Roughly speaking, radiocarbon dating relies on the fact that when any living thing dies, it ceases to absorb carbon from the environment and the amount of the isotope ^{12}C remains constant, whereas the radioactive ^{14}C isotope decays at a predictable rate, thus allowing scientists to assess the date of plant, animal, or human remains in the archaeological record on the basis of the ratio between the remaining quantities of ^{12}C and ^{14}C isotopes. However, because the amount of radiocarbon in the earth's atmosphere is not constant over time (a fact that Libby and Ward did not initially recognize), the raw radiocarbon dates all have to be calibrated by a technique using radiocarbon-dated samples taken from long sequences of tree-rings of known date, from very long-living species of tree, such as the sequoia and the bristlecone pine. The use of this so-called 'calibration curve' to convert radiocarbon dates into real absolute ones means that scientists don't tend to be able to give a single absolute date, but rather they express the percentage of likelihood that the real date lies within a particular span of years. To give an actual example, a sample of pomegranate seeds from an 18th-Dynasty burial reusing a 5th-Dynasty tomb at Saqqara produced a raw date of 3195 BP (i.e. 3195 radiocarbon years before AD 1950), which, in conventional terms, is equivalent to 1245 BC. The radiocarbon date was then calibrated, producing a 68.2 per cent likelihood that the 'real' absolute date lay somewhere between 1498 and 1437 BC (which actually agrees very well with the estimates of dates for the 18th-Dynasty pottery and other artefacts found along with the seeds).

Despite the fact that Egyptian objects played such a crucial role in the early development of radiocarbon dating itself, it is only comparatively recently that scientific dating of this kind has begun to be seriously incorporated into Egyptian chronology. For many years the technique has been under-used by historians of ancient Egypt not only because of a misguided perception that the traditional chronology required very little help from science (and that the margins of error on radiocarbon dates were excessive compared to traditional dates), but also for the more practical reason that it has been almost impossible for most researchers to gain official permission to take samples out of Egypt for dating. Since there are few radiocarbon dating facilities within Egypt itself, opportunities for systematic radiocarbon dating of Egyptian material have been extremely limited. Nevertheless, in 2001 permission was given for systematic radiocarbon dating of over 450 Egyptian Old and Middle Kingdom samples in order to see how well they correlated with the traditional chronology. The results showed an intriguing mixture of correlations and discrepancies, but initially little attempt was made to assess the implications of these new calibrated dates. About a decade later, two new major dating projects (one in Oxford, and another in Vienna) were published—strikingly, however, they came up with very different overall results.

The Oxford project was the first major application of the so-called 'Bayesian' statistical method to radiocarbon dates from Egypt. The method uses not only dendrochronology but also all kinds of other contextual chronological data (such as the order in which individual kings reigned, and the traditional estimates of lengths of their reigns), in order to enhance the calibration process. The Oxford team reached the conclusion that their 200+ radiocarbon dates (all taken on short-lived material types, such as papyrus, mostly from very secure archaeological contexts) were broadly inline with the traditional 'high' chronology, i.e. the version of the traditional Egyptian chronology that opts for slightly earlier dates. For the Middle Kingdom, for instance, the Oxford radiocarbon-based chronology seemed to validate the conventional assumption of a date of *c*.1872 BC for the observation of a heliacal rising of Sirius in the reign of Senusret III.

The results of the Vienna project were more problematic. Working with samples from Manfred Bietak's excavations of the Second Intermediate Period city and cemeteries at Tell el-Dab'a (see Chapter 2), they found that the radiocarbon dates diverged quite significantly from Bietak's own dates, which were based on such archaeological factors as stratigraphy, pottery seriations, and synchronisms with other Near Eastern and Mediterranean chronological sequences. There is absolutely no doubt that radiocarbon dating is finally beginning to have a more serious impact on Egyptian chronology and history, but there are clearly still issues to be resolved (and these are almost certainly issues connected with the traditional methods of chronology-building rather than with the radiocarbon dates!).

Historical change and material culture

One of the most effective dating methods used by modern Egyptologists is the study of the styles and fabrics of pottery vessels, not least because fragments of pottery make up the vast majority of material from Egyptian archaeological sites. There has been an enormous growth in the study of Egyptian pottery in the last fifty years, both with regard to the quantity of sherds being analysed (from a wide variety of types of site) and in terms of the range of scientific techniques now being used to extract more information from ceramics. Inevitably the improvement in our understanding of this prolific aspect of Egyptian material culture has had an impact on the chronological framework.

The way ahead in construction of Egyptian chronologies must surely lie in this kind of research. King-lists and the like can only tell us about limited aspects of political change (the rise and fall of dynasties and individual rulers), whereas chronological frameworks based on particular elements of Egyptian material culture from sites throughout the country can provide information on the history of ancient Egyptian society and economy. Many modern histories of ancient Egypt therefore increasingly focus as much on social and cultural developments—such as evolving settlement patterns, exploitation and manufacture of different materials, and changes in diet and health—as on the traditional fare of kings, queens, and dynasties.

Chapter 4
Writing

Egyptian hieroglyphs consist of ideograms (signs employed as direct representations of phenomena such as 'sky' ⚏ or 'man' 𓀀) as well as phonetic signs representing the sound of all or part of a spoken word. The connections between writing and art were therefore much stronger in pharaonic Egypt than in many other cultures. In the hieroglyphic script decorating buildings and sculptures, the writing of simple words such as 'goose' 𓅬 or 'head' 𓁶 was to some extent an artistic exercise as well as an act of verbal communication. A third type of hieroglyph is the 'determinative', which is so-called because it 'determines' (i.e. categorizes) the meaning of the entire word. Thus, for example, a variety of words referring to movement conclude with a determinative comprising a pair of walking legs (𓂻), and more abstract words, such as 'to know', are followed by a determinative in the form of a rolled up papyrus (𓏛), indicating that these words are concerned with thought and intellect.

Many of the surviving texts from ancient Egypt were created in order to complement and annotate the paintings and reliefs decorating the surfaces of the walls and ceilings of temples and tombs. Both the appearance and function of Egyptian writing and art were therefore closely connected with religious beliefs and funerary practices, and the Egyptians appear to have believed strongly in the real physical potency of words and images. Indeed, in many inscriptions on tomb-walls or funerary equipment, it was considered necessary to remove certain portions of hieroglyphs, such as the legs of bird-signs, in order to incapacitate forces that might prove malevolent to the deceased. This sense of the magical potential of verbal and artistic representations was expressed in the funerary ritual known as the 'opening of the mouth', with which both the mummies and statues of the deceased were thought to be imbued with new life—a variant of this ritual seems to have been performed each morning in Ptolemaic temples in order to bring to life the texts and images on the walls.

The Narmer Palette and the origins of Egyptian writing

Like many early artefacts, the Narmer Palette includes symbols that have been interpreted either as purely pictorial elements, as strings of unconnected pictograms, or even as organized, grammatical sentences. What does this tell us about current views concerning the origins and nature of writing in Egypt?

The pictorial narrative on the palette appears to be complemented by early hieroglyphs such as the 'catfish' and 'chisel' signs that hover in front of the smiting figure of the king. These two signs have the phonetic values *nar* and *mer* respectively in pharaonic times, but it is not clear whether the signs on the palette are being used phonetically or ideogrammatically. Some scholars have suggested that the signs should actually be read as Nar-mehet because the hieroglyphic sign 'chisel' might be phonetically interpreted not as *mr* ('chisel') but *mḥr* ('aggressive'). The king's name would then mean 'aggressive catfish', which perhaps makes better sense.

The king's name is repeated at the top of each side of the palette, framed in a *serekh*, which was a powerful symbol of kingship, probably representing the entrance to an early royal palace. We know that this *serekh* symbol was used from the late Predynastic period onwards as a way of framing and indicating one of the king's names (known to Egyptologists as his 'Horus name' because the *serekh* often has a Horus falcon perched protectively over it). There are, however, also a number of other signs on this side of the palette, which most Egyptologists interpret as early hieroglyphs (see description in Chapter 1 above). Opinions differ as to whether the four symbols at the top right of this side of the palette (immediately above the ten decapitated bodies) are hieroglyphs or pictures.

In 1961, Alan Gardiner went so far as to describe the palette's decoration (and particularly the group of symbols hovering in front of the face of the smiting Narmer) as a 'complex of pictures which the spectator would then translate into words'. In 1991, however, Walter Fairservis Jr published an article setting out an even more philological interpretation. He argued that previous Egyptologists' interpretations of the Narmer Palette had been subject to 'a significant methodological flaw' because they had treated most of the decorated surface of the palette as pictorial rather than linguistic. Fairservis took the highly controversial view that all of the symbols on both sides of the palette should be translated into grammatical phrases, written in a very early version of the Egyptian hieroglyphic system. In other words, he argued that, instead of interpreting the palette as a combination of art and writing, it should be literally *read* as one long sentence. He identified sixty-two putative 'hieroglyphs', and discussed the possible nuances of meaning contained in each of them, then assembled them into a form of text, on the basis of which he claimed that the palette was 'not documentation of the unification of Upper and Lower Egypt, but instead represents a victory by the leader of the Edfu district over the Nile valley south into Nubia'. This theory is not generally accepted by other Egyptologists, but it does raise the question of the extent to which late Predynastic and Early Dynastic art includes fully developed writing of the spoken language, as opposed to conveying information through purely artistic images.

Recent studies on the origins of the Egyptian writing system have focused on several specific questions. When did the hieroglyphic system first begin to be used, and when did it begin to incorporate phonetics and grammar? Was it adopted from another culture (the most likely candidate being the Near East, where writing seems to have emerged in Mesopotamia at a slightly earlier date), or did it emerge independently in Egypt, and if so could it have been 'invented' by a single individual or a small group of innovators, as opposed to evolving slowly over a number of generations or centuries?

Another question that tends to be asked about all early writing systems is whether they emerged through practical bureaucratic requirements or whether their initial development was much more concerned with ritualistic and ceremonial purposes. Were the earliest Egyptian hieroglyphs a kind of propagandist tool used by rulers and elite groups to preserve their own power? The answer to this question is complicated by the fact that our views of the dates at which writing emerged in different cultures, and also the purposes for which it was initially used, are very much determined by the kinds of materials used as writing media (e.g. clay tablets, bone and ivory labels, rolls of papyrus, and stone monuments), and by their ability to survive in the environmental conditions that prevail in different parts of the world. Because the clay tablets used for administrative records in early Mesopotamia were well preserved by the local conditions, they gave the impression, to some scholars, that writing had emerged to serve bureaucratic purposes, whereas in Mesoamerica, China, and Egypt, it appeared that the earliest inscribed objects (such as Maya stone stelae and Egyptian stone palettes) were used for ceremonial purposes, primarily concerned with the maintenance of power by an elite group. This cross-cultural view of writing of course ignores the fact that, by their very nature, administrative archives in most early societies will tend to have been inscribed on cheaper, less durable materials (such as papyrus in Egypt, which is known to have been in use as early as the 1st Dynasty). Such low-cost bureaucratic materials will therefore not tend to survive very well, whereas the earliest ceremonial and 'propagandist' texts are characteristically written on highly durable materials (primarily stone), which are far more likely to have survived. Of course, it might also be argued that the idea of making a binary distinction between administrative and ceremonial/propagandist texts is a slightly dubious one, and that textual genres may be particularly difficult to characterize at the time that ancient texts are first emerging.

What do we know about the very beginning of Egyptian writing?

The general assumption, until comparatively recently, was that the first examples of the Sumerian cuneiform writing system appeared significantly earlier than the Egyptian hieroglyphs. It was therefore further assumed that the first Egyptian texts, which seemed to have emerged relatively abruptly at the end of the 4th millennium BC, were probably inspired by increased Egyptian links with the Near East. However, the actual signs making up the two systems (Sumerian cuneiform and Old Egyptian hieroglyphs) are so different that it seems highly unlikely that the Egyptian system evolved directly out of cuneiform. This does not mean, however, that the basic *idea* of pictographic writing could not have emerged from Mesopotamia and simply been emulated in a more general sense.

These assumptions were somewhat unravelled by archaeological discoveries made by German archaeologists at Abydos during the 1990s, which suggested not only that the hieroglyphic script might have already begun to be used in the middle of the Predynastic period (at least as early as 3300 BC), but also that the use of phonetic signs might have appeared much earlier than previously thought. The excavations at tomb U-j, the impressive burial of a ruler called Scorpion (evidently an earlier Scorpion than the owner of the mace-head found near the Narmer Palette) revealed

10. Labels from tomb U-j at Abydos, bearing early hieroglyph-style symbols, c.3300 BC.

one room containing about 150 small ivory labels that appear to bear clearly recognizable hieroglyphs including numbers, commodities, and possibly also place-names or royal agricultural estates (Figure 10). The importance of these labels is that they are perhaps not just inscribed with pictorial signs ('ideograms'), which would represent a much more basic stage in the history of the script. Instead, many of them may be representations of sounds in the spoken language ('phonograms'), a stage in the development of the script that was not thought to have occurred until at least the 1st Dynasty. The German philologists who studied the labels identified them as phonetic symbols because they often appear to spell out the names of well-known towns frequently mentioned in later inscriptions, such as Buto and Bubastis. Not all Egyptologists agree with these interpretations of the symbols carved onto the labels, but most would agree with the basic premise that they are at least some form of proto-script, and that their purpose was to communicate meaning through symbols. In a recent discussion of the origins of Egyptian hieroglyphs, Andréas Stauder takes a minimalist view of the significance of the U-j labels, arguing that they 'do not…evidence representation of language, and are best interpreted as a non-linguistic marked system', although he does acknowledge that the inscriptions display some important features of writing, such as regimentation of forms, orientation, and miniaturization.

Notwithstanding Stauder's caution, it appears that some of the craftsmen employed by the earliest rulers at Abydos—at least 200 years before the 1st Dynasty—were already using a sophisticated form of symbolic communication, perhaps involving phonetic signs as well as ideograms. Culturally speaking, the fact that this writing may often refer to Lower Egyptian place-names as the sources of goods placed in an Upper Egyptian ruler's tomb is also very strong evidence that the northern and southern halves of Egypt were already closely connected economically—and perhaps politically too. Thus, many of the factors conventionally associated with fully developed states—such as writing, bureaucracy, monumental architecture, and complex systems of exchange and economic control—were evidently in place in Egypt at a time when the culture was, until comparatively recently, conventionally regarded as 'prehistoric'.

Use and abuse of texts in Egyptology

The beginning of Egyptology as a complete historical discipline, combining the study of both texts and archaeology, was made possible by Champollion's decipherment of Egyptian hieroglyphs in 1822. By the late 1820s, the demotic script had also been deciphered (largely by Thomas Young)—thus, within a single decade, ancient Egyptian culture had been dragged from prehistory into history. By the 1860s, Charles Goodwin and François Chabas had deciphered and translated many papyri inscribed with the hieratic script, thus ensuring that texts in all four Egyptian scripts—hieroglyphics, hieratic, demotic, and Coptic—could now be understood. Coptic, the last phase of the ancient Egyptian language (still spoken at least as recently as the

10th century AD), has of course survived into modern times, in written form, as the liturgical language of the Coptic Church.

Almost from the moment that hieroglyphs, hieratic, and demotic began to be translated, research into pharaonic Egypt was increasingly characterized by a struggle to reconcile the kinds of general socio-economic evidence preserved in the archaeological record with the more specific historical information contained in ancient texts. While the newly discovered knowledge of the texts had the potential to revive the very thoughts and emotions of the ancient Egyptians, it also introduced a temptation to assume that the answers to questions about Egyptian civilization could be found in the written word rather than the archaeologist's trench. The purely archaeological view of Egyptian culture, as it was preserved in the form of buried walls, artefacts, and organic remains, would henceforth always have to be seen in the context of a richly detailed corpus of texts written on stone, clay, and papyrus. In Egyptian archaeology, as in other historical disciplines, the written word, with all its potential for subjectivity and persuasion, can have a paradoxical tendency to obscure—and sometimes even eclipse—the physical archaeological evidence.

It is interesting, from the point of view of the dichotomy between texts and archaeology, to compare the history of Egyptian archaeology with that of modern Maya studies. Mayanists appear to have experienced the reverse situation: their discipline was predominantly anthropological and archaeological until Maya glyphs began to be deciphered in the 1980s, producing a sudden flood of texts in the Mayan language, which have significantly altered the perception of the Maya culture. The suspicion with which Maya archaeologists initially regarded the historical information provided by their philological colleagues presents a mirror-image of the reaction of many traditional text-based Egyptologists to the increasingly science-based and anthropological analyses of pharaonic Egypt produced by archaeologists in recent years. Both Mayanists and Egyptologists are struggling to come to terms with the basic fact that writing tends to be the product of elite members of society whereas the bulk of archaeological data derives from the illiterate majority of the population; the solution lies in the successful integration of these types of evidence to produce a view of society as a whole.

There have, in the past, been many syntheses of ancient Egyptian textual and archaeological material, but increasingly, as the sheer amount of both types of data continues to grow, linguists and archaeologists seem to have taken somewhat divergent paths. In a discussion of the administration of Nubia in the Middle Kingdom, employing both textual and archaeological data, Barry Kemp argues that textual sources usually only reveal 'fragments of systems', often lacking a sense of physical and cultural context, whereas archaeology can suggest the 'broad structural outlines in society'. Nevertheless, there is no doubt that Egyptian textual evidence is often able to supply those personal details that help to transform abstract socio-economic processes into something that is closer to conventional history. Often the problem is that archaeological and textual data are analysed and interpreted entirely separately, rather than being blended and fused into more holistic views of Egyptian culture and history.

Chapter 5
Kingship

Both of the faces of the Narmer Palette are decorated with warlike scenes of the king, but it is the large depiction of the king smiting a foreigner with his mace on the reverse of the palette that is probably the most potent image. The royal smiting scene is one of the most common images in Egyptian art, serving as a metaphor for the power of the pharaoh, who preserves the order of the universe by ritually subduing the forces of chaos. In 1899, the year after the discovery of the Narmer Palette itself, an earlier Predynastic version of the smiting scene was found by Frederick Green at Hierakonpolis, on the wall of Tomb 100—the first surviving Egyptian tomb to contain painted decoration. This burial seems to have been created for a local ruler at around 3600 BC (i.e. the Naqada IIC phase of the Predynastic). Almost a century later, in the 1990s, an even earlier example of the motif, showing a tall figure smiting three crouching captives, was found painted on a pottery vessel excavated from the Predynastic tomb U-239 at Abydos (dated to the late Naqada I period, c.3800 BC). The classic icon of the smiting pharaoh retained its significance for thousands of years, appearing in a variety of religious and artistic contexts, from amulets and stelae to the walls and pylons of temples as late as the Roman period.

One theme that repeatedly appears in Egyptological studies is the nature of the Egyptian king, and particularly his relationship both with his fellow mortals and with the Egyptian pantheon. The Narmer Palette already establishes a close link between the king and the falcon-god Horus, with its depiction of the divine falcon holding a foreign captive in front of Narmer. The interaction between king and god in the act of conquest conveys some of the complexity of the symbolism and metaphors surrounding the ancient Egyptian conceptions of kingship. The idea of the despotic pharaoh has found its way into the modern consciousness via many different means, from the Bible to Shelley, and Egyptologists have frequently used the debate concerning Egyptian kingship to explore such topics as the changing nature of the Egyptian political system, and the question of what we can know of the identities of the various pharaohs as real individuals (as opposed to iconographical ciphers). In the case of Egyptian rulers, so many of their mummified bodies have survived (especially from the New Kingdom) that we are in the unusual position of being able actually to gaze into their faces as if they were our contemporaries, while simultaneously examining the long-ruined monuments and surviving texts from their reigns.

For the Egyptians, the reign of each new king represented a new beginning, not merely philosophically but practically, given the fact that dates were expressed in the form of the 'regnal years' of each individual ruler. This means that there would probably have been a psychological tendency to regard each new reign as a fresh point of origin. Every king was essentially reworking the same universal myths of kingship within the events of his own time. By the late Old Kingdom, every king held five names (the so-called 'fivefold titulary'), each of which encapsulated a particular aspect of the kingship: three of them stressed his role as a god, while the other two emphasized the supposed division of Egypt into two unified lands.

Many rulers held the titles 'mighty bull' and 'bull of Horus' (both of the depictions of Narmer on the palette show him wearing a bull's tail hanging from his waist as part of the royal regalia). The figure of the bull trampling a fallen foreigner and breaking through the walls of a city, depicted on the lower part of the front of the Narmer Palette, is probably symbolic of the king's victory over foreign territories. This strong identification between king and bull continued throughout the pharaonic period. There was perhaps an element of punning involved in the king/bull correlation, in that the Egyptian term for bull was *ka*, which was phonetically identical to another word often used to refer to the king's divine counterpart or 'double'.

A great deal of metaphor and symbolism was involved in the kings' names and iconography. This has made it difficult for modern scholars to use these kinds of evidence to arrive at a sense of the individual characteristics and activities of particular kings, as opposed to the general idea of kingship. In reading Egyptologists' accounts of the reigns of various pharaohs, we have to consider two kinds of stereotyping and pigeonholing: first, the ancient stereotypes that the original Egyptian texts present us with and, second, the unconscious contemporary stereotyping of which Egyptologists themselves are sometimes guilty.

Athletes and proto-feminists?

One particular 'victim' of regal stereotyping was the 18th-Dynasty ruler Amenhotep II, who is repeatedly portrayed on his monuments as a real sporting hero. Alan Gardiner, in 1961, described him as follows:

> His muscular strength was extraordinary: we are told that he can shoot at a metal target of one palm's thickness and pierce it in such a way that his arrow would stick out on the other side; unhappily the like had been related of Thutmose III, though with less detail, so that we are not without excuse for scepticism. Nonetheless there are other examples of his athletic prowess too individual to be rejected out of hand.

In the 1980s, the French Egyptologist Nicolas Grimal even saw these traits in Amenhotep's names and epithets, such as his Horus and Golden Horus names ('powerful bull with great strength' and 'he who seizes all the lands by strength' respectively). The problem of whether Amenhotep II was actually an unusually athletic king, however, is much more a question of unpicking formulaic details from idiosyncratic facts.

First, is it simply a case of accident of survival, whereby more texts concerning athleticism happen to have been preserved from the time of Amenhotep II than from other reigns? Second, if it is not an accident of survival, do we interpret this as an indication that the king was actually a great sportsman or do we simply credit him with making an enormous contribution to the *idea* of the Egyptian king being a great athlete?

When confronted by the question of individual pharaohs' distinctive personalities, as preserved in the visual and textual record, many Egyptologists, and a number of other scholars, have naturally been tempted to speculate as to their characters and motivations. This second question in particular leads us inevitably to the much-caricatured Hatshepsut, one of a very small group of women (perhaps five altogether over a period of thousands of years) who managed to rule Egypt in their own right, rather than as appendages of male rulers.

The term 'queen' is frequently applied to royal females in Egypt but Egyptologists use it at their peril, since there is no real ancient Egyptian word for an independent female ruler, only a few phrases used to describe women related by blood or marriage to the ruling male (principally the 'great royal wife' (*ḥmt wrt nsw*), the 'royal mother' (*mwt nsw*), and the 'royal wives' (*ḥmwt nsw*)). This meant that in those rare situations when women became 'kings' themselves, they were virtually obliged to adopt male regalia and attributes. Certainly Hatshepsut, who is the female ruler for whom

11. Image of Thutmose III (left) making offerings to a statue of Queen Hatshepsut in the form of the male god Osiris (right), from the Red Chapel at Karnak, c.1473–1458 BC.

most evidence has survived, had herself portrayed for much of her reign as if she were physically male (Figure 11). In her cult temple at Deir el-Bahari and in other monuments she is frequently shown in male kingly costume, including the royal 'false beard'. There must presumably have been some sense of conflict between her sex and the masculine role of the pharaoh, but only the posthumous erasures of her name from monuments have survived as indications of such feelings of inappropriateness. Interestingly, her royal names and titles are regularly written with feminine grammatical endings (and one of them perhaps deliberately recalls one of the names of the Middle Kingdom female ruler Sobekneferu), producing a set of wordplays connecting her with certain deities and aspects of divinity that would have not been possible within a male king's nomenclature.

Almost certainly because of Hatshepsut's gender, there has been a tendency for many Egyptologists to stereotype her as a pacifist. Nicholas Grimal's history of Egypt, published in the 1980s, argued that her only real foray into the outside world was the trading mission to the land of Punt:

> This expedition [to Punt], recounted in great detail on the walls of Hatshepsut's mortuary temple, represented the high point of a foreign policy that was limited to the exploitation of the Wadi Maghara mines in Sinai and the despatch of one military expedition into Nubia . . . During the reign of Hatshepsut the only military actions were to consolidate the achievements of Thutmose I . . .

In the 1960s, however, the Canadian Egyptologist Donald Redford had already put forward a revisionist view of the queen's reign, suggesting that unjustified assumptions were being made on the basis of an apparent absence of evidence rather than actual facts. He makes the point that some male rulers, such as Horemheb and Shoshenq I, might be wrongly regarded as pacifists if the same conclusions were drawn on the basis of a paucity of texts describing military expeditions. In the case of Horemheb, we have ample evidence from his pre-royal career as Tutankhamun's general to know that he was anything but a pacifist.

Another debate concerning the reign and personality of Hatshepsut centres on the two closely connected questions of whether she was a weak ruler who used an unusual amount of propaganda to bolster her claims to the throne and whether she was unusually influenced by her (male) steward Senenmut. We therefore find Redford suggesting in 1967 that:

> There can be no doubt that her chief supporter was her steward Senenmut, a man of low origin, who throughout most of her reign

appears to have been something of a power behind the throne...
She had a circle of favourites, a motley collection of individuals with
no common background and little reason to share political goals.

Redford goes on to argue that Hatshepsut was then gradually
eclipsed as Thutmose III began to appear more often in reliefs
and was delegated the task of undertaking foreign wars—however,
none of this was different from any other coregency between a
king and his successor: Egyptian princes generally were given
greater prominence in order to prepare them for the kingship.

Fortunately the French Egyptologist Suzanne Ratié presents a
much more nuanced view of Hatshepsut's relationship with
Senenmut:

> The personality of Senenmut was therefore rich and complex.
> Certain aspects of his career are impenetrable. It seems that his
> influence is visible in all the great achievements of the reign at least
> until year 16. It is difficult to differentiate the role played by the
> queen and her 'adviser' in various decisions and activities. We use
> the term 'adviser' to describe Senenmut, but we deliberately avoid
> the use of the term 'favourite', for this aspect of the lives of
> Hatshepsut and Senenmut is completely out of our reach and does
> not rest on any objective evidence.

Finally, a third historical debate concerning Hatshepsut centres
on a relief in her mortuary temple at Deir el-Bahari that appears
to justify her right to the throne by portraying her birth as the
result of sexual intercourse between the god Amun and her
human mother, Ahmose. There are a very small number of royal
monuments from the New Kingdom that also contain claims that
the ruler in question was the result of sexual intercourse between
a deity and a woman (e.g. the scenes of the divine birth of
Amenhotep III at Luxor), thus suggesting that the ruler was
physically semi-divine. It is possible that such scenes might
originally have been standard parts of many royal monuments,

and that it is only by chance that they have survived from certain reigns and not others. However, it is also possible—as many Egyptologists have argued—that some rulers were more concerned to stress their legitimacy than others.

Egyptologists have frequently speculated as to whether these so-called 'scenes of divine birth' of Hatshepsut and Amenhotep III, at Deir el-Bahari and Luxor temple respectively, were propagandistic or religious documents (or perhaps both at the same time). It has been frequently argued that Hatshepsut's gender forced her to come up with new methods of justifying her position. But this does not explain why Amenhotep III (and later also Ramesses II, in some less substantial surviving scenes) should have felt the need to utilize the myth of divine birth when none of Hatshepsut's 'gender problems' applied. In *The Miraculous Birth of King Amon-hotep III and Other Egyptian Studies* (1912) Colin Campbell argued that the reasons for the birth scenes of both Hatshepsut and Amenhotep III were largely religious rather than political, being concerned with the replacement of the cult of Ra in the kingship by that of Amun, so that the aim was to establish the king as the son of Amun rather than the son of the sun-god Ra. It has been pointed out, however, that Amun was already being described as the king's father as early as the reign of Ahmose, three generations before Hatshepsut. Essentially the question of Hatshepsut's motivation for stressing her divine birth remains uncertain.

Although patchy data can always lead to interpretative problems, there can be little doubt that these three problems with late 20th-century interpretations of the reign of Hatshepsut derive at least partly from Egyptologists' assumptions and personal prejudices, which cause them not only to interpret the evidence in misleading ways but to deliberately build up semi-fictionalized images of the female ruler, no doubt bringing to the topic a wide range of (largely inappropriate) later female royal stereotypes from Western history, such as Elizabeth I, Victoria, and even Catherine the Great.

Apart from Hatshepsut, two other Egyptian 'queens' who have received the full treatment in posthumous personality profiling are Nefertiti (one of whose sculptures has become a kind of celebrity in its own right) and Cleopatra VII, the last of the Ptolemaic rulers and a considerable cinematic icon. I will discuss the reputations and multifarious influences of Nefertiti and Cleopatra in Chapter 9 (Egyptomania), since these two Egyptian queens have undoubtedly crossed over into the arena of modern popular culture.

Ramesses the Great

A considerably more conventional—but nevertheless still stereotyped—view of Egyptian kingship is encountered in the case of Ramesses II, who seems to have begun to be regarded as some kind of archetype even in his own lifetime. He was evidently much admired (and envied) by his successors, such as Ramesses III, who, only thirty years after his more illustrious predecessor's death, not only dedicated a chapel to the deified Ramesses II at Medinet Habu, but also gave his own sons the same names as Ramesses II's sons.

By the 11th century BC Ramesses II had become such a powerful mythological figure that one 11st Dynasty Book of the Dead papyrus (British Museum EA75026) attempted to gain extra potency by identifying itself as 'the writing which was found on the neck of the mummy of King Usimare (Ramesses II)'. It is also clear that Ramesses had become very closely associated with the institution of Egyptian kingship itself from the fact that, in the Third Intermediate Period, priests and high officials were sometimes given the title 'King's son of Ramesses', showing the great power of the name Ramesses alone.

Ramesses II's memory would live on in later traditions both under his own name and under that of Sesostris (the latter being the name of several Middle Kingdom rulers whose monuments Ramesses had usurped during his lifetime, and whose reputations were also inexorably absorbed into his own). In the 5th century BC, Herodotus described a character called Rhampsinitus, whom he credits with the building of the gateways at the western end of the precinct of Ptah at Memphis, also suggesting that he was a frequent visitor to the underworld. In his *Histories* (Book 2, sections 121–3), Herodotus describes two events in the reign of Rhampsinitus, who seems to be a semi-mythologized mixture of Ramesses II and III. The first is an account of how the king played dice in the underworld, and the second tells of a cunning theft from the king's treasury and his attempts to thwart the thieves.

About 400 years later, in the early 1st century BC, Diodorus Siculus describes a monument that he calls the 'tomb of Osymandias'. This appears to be the Ramesseum, Ramesses II's mortuary temple in western Thebes, and the name Osymandias was a Hellenicization of User-maat-ra, Ramesses II's prenomen. A version of this name appeared again in 1817, when Percy Bysshe Shelley published a sonnet called 'Ozymandias' that included the famous lines: 'My name is Ozymandias, king of kings: look on my works ye mighty, and despair!' Shelley in fact never visited Egypt and was probably inspired by visits to the British Museum. A few months before he wrote the Ozymandias sonnet he had spent an evening with John Keats and James Henry Leigh Hunt writing poems about the River Nile. The poem is clearly indebted to Diodorus Siculus, and Shelley had perhaps also read William Hamilton's guidebook to Egypt, *Aegyptiaca*, published in 1809. It is also probably significant that it was in 1817 that the British Museum received part of a colossal statue of Ramesses called the Younger Memnon, brought back from the second court of the Ramesseum by Belzoni as a gift from Mohammed Ali to the prince regent.

Ramesses has also enjoyed a rich fictional afterlife, with a sequence of novels written about him by the Egyptologist-turned-novelist Christian Jacq in the 1990s, as well as Ann Rice's *The Mummy or Ramesses the Damned* (1989), in which Ramesses is resurrected by a magic elixir (along with Cleopatra).

The approach to Ramesses II, from the late New Kingdom through to 20th-century accounts of his life and reign, seems to have been to allow him to serve as a kind of amalgam of the classic traits of arrogance and despotism that tend to be regarded as appropriate to Egyptian kingship. Finally, one of Ramesses' most even-handed biographers, Kenneth Kitchen, attempts to protect Ramesses from such careless typecasting, but in the process seems to create a rather genial monarch. Criticizing his fellow Egyptologists for their pigeonholing of Ramesses, he speculates as to what the king would make of the modern world:

Initially, perhaps, he would be dazzled by the technology and sciences . . . But before very long he would see through the material façade and (in quest of Maat) perceive also the reverse of the coin in a world cursed with exactly the same basic human rivalries and failings that he knew in his own world . . . Finally he would doubtless also see the abiding positive values of love, devotion, regard for right, a certain mutual tolerance on non essentials . . .

If the traditional despotic view of Ramesses is disturbing, then how much more disturbing is Kitchen's concept of Ramesses as a kind of archbishop of Canterbury?

For a genuine dose of realism on the stereotypes of Egyptian kingship, we should perhaps turn to Jan Assman, who (in *The Search for God in Ancient Egypt*) describes the way in which kingship seems to lie at the heart of Egyptian creation myths:

The starting point was the king. He was the incarnation of the god Horus, the son who ever and again has to overcome the death of his father to gain his throne. The Ennead [group of nine creation deities] before whom he must prove that he is the rightful heir to the throne is both his family and the cosmos itself; read in descending order, his genealogy is a cosmogony.

This passage gives some sense of the context of most of the texts and images that have survived from the reigns of Amenhotep II, Hatshepsut, and Ramesses II, and with all this cosmic imagery, we should be grateful that we can catch any faint glimpses of individuality and personality from the sources. If Egyptian rulers sound arrogant, this is because they were obliged to see themselves, at least in theory, as the linchpins of humanity and the universe.

Chapter 6
Identity

The Narmer Palette includes scenes in which either the king himself or his divine alter-egos (the falcon-god Horus on one side and a bull on the other) dispatch or humiliate foreigners and enemies. As we have seen, these images are part of the paraphernalia of Egyptian stereotypical kingship, but they are also part of the iconography through which the ancient Egyptian population perhaps defined and reaffirmed themselves as a people and as a nation, in contrast to what they saw as the chaotic sea of foreignness that lay beyond their borders. It is unclear whether the figure held in captivity by the Horus falcon on the Narmer Palette was a Libyan or an Asiatic, or whether this was a case of civil war and the prisoner is a Lower Egyptian, in the process of being forcibly integrated into a united Upper and Lower Egyptian kingdom. We might also ask whether the two prone figures in the lower part of the palette, and also the ten decapitated and emasculated human figures on the other side of the palette, are Lower Egyptians or foreigners. Did Upper Egyptians regard Lower Egyptians as quasi-foreigners during the final phase of the Predynastic? Were the king and his courtiers not 'Egyptian' themselves but invaders from the Near East, as Egyptologists such as Petrie and Emery argued? If so, which figures on the palette were the true Egyptians?

The iconography of Egypt's early ethnic identity

It seems in fact that the Narmer Palette may have a particular significance with regard to the early pharaonic Egyptians' definition of their own national identity. As far as we know, Narmer is the last ruler to be depicted as an animated version of the creature after which he is named: hence Narmer's ivory label and cylinder seal (see Chapter 3) both show a somewhat improbably anthropomorphized catfish in the act of smiting foreign captives, whereas the palette bears not only the bestial symbols of pharaoh as falcon and bull, but also the image of the smiting human figure of the king.

Questions of identity undoubtedly pervade the Narmer Palette just as they permeate the study of ancient Egypt as a whole. What was it like to be an ancient Egyptian, and how did they distinguish themselves from neighbouring peoples? Were they a distinctively African civilization or one of several variants of standard Near Eastern culture? Should we define them by their language, their geographical location, or their physical appearance? How did they see themselves? In many ways the Egyptians defined themselves and their rulers by establishing and emphasizing sharp contrasts with non-Egyptians in Africa and the Near East. The regions with which Egypt gradually fostered commercial and political links can be grouped into three basic areas: Africa (primarily Nubia, Libya, and Punt), Asia (Syria–Palestine, Mesopotamia, Arabia, and Anatolia), and the northern and eastern Mediterranean (Cyprus, Crete, the Sea Peoples, and the Greeks).

The Narmer Palette may also have something to say about early Egyptian contact with the outside world. In 1955, an analysis by the Israeli archaeologist Yigael Yadin led to the suggestion that the Narmer Palette might not simply be a series of scenes celebrating kingly power or ritual, nor even, as the older theories suggested, a narrative of the unification of Egypt. Instead, Yadin argued that it might show early Egyptian military conflict with the Near East. He focused on the two prone figures below the large smiting figure of King Narmer. These two human figures appear to be identified in some way by a pair of hieroglyph-like signs. The left-hand sign seems to be the rectangular outline of a fortified enclosure, while the right-hand one, if it is also an architectural image, might be seen as a semi-circular enclosure with two walls fanning out from it. Yadin suggests that this right-hand sign might be the Egyptians' rendition of a peculiar kite-shaped enclosure (i.e. diamond-shaped, with a pair of hanging 'strings', when viewed from above), built by nomadic pastoralists. Many examples of these buildings have survived in the Hamad desert near the modern city of Amman, where they are thought to have served as fortified enclosures into which animals could be herded in order to protect them from raiding parties. If these two architectural images identify the places of origin of the two figures, the first may represent the fortified enclosures that might have been encountered by Egyptians campaigning in Early Bronze Age Palestine, and the second may portray the kite-like structures associated with the nomadic pastoralists of the Trans-Jordanian region.

Interestingly enough, excavations at the Early Bronze Age I sites of Tel Erani and Arad, in Israel, have revealed Egyptian potsherds bearing the name of Narmer written in a *serekh* frame, along with many other Egyptian artefacts, including prestige items such as mace-heads, of similar date. This suggests that there was certainly a strong Egyptian presence in Palestine in the late 4th millennium BC, which might therefore provide some archaeological support for Yadin's theory of very early Egyptian military expansion into the Levant.

Egyptian ethnicities and controversies

How did the Egyptians view themselves? We can try to answer this question first by looking at the way in which they portrayed themselves in painting and sculpture, and second by analysing their depictions of 'foreigners'. As in many other cultures, the Egyptians seem to have gained a sense of their own identity primarily by contrasting themselves with the peoples of the world outside their borders. Scenes in the tombs of the New Kingdom pharaohs Seti I and Ramesses III in the Valley of the Kings specifically depict the various human types in the universe over which the sun-god Ra presided. Although partly based on skin colour and other physical characteristics, these different ethnicities were also based on varieties in hairstyles and costume, and their function was apparently to allow the Egyptians to define themselves as a national group, relative to the rest of the world. Such depictions, however, would have been recognized by the Egyptians themselves as simplified stereotypes, given that the thousands of portrayals of individual Egyptians show that the population as a whole ranged across a heterogeneous spectrum of ethnicities, as in Egypt today.

There is, therefore, also a sense in which the ancient 'Egyptians' regarded themselves as a distinct population in purely *cultural* terms. There are many examples of individuals whom Egyptians regarded as identical to themselves in social and political terms, despite the fact that they were obviously 'foreign' in their physical appearance. One good example of this is Maiherpri, a military official in the early 18th Dynasty who was granted the great privilege of a tomb in the Valley of the Kings but whose physical features clearly indicate that he was of Nubian extraction. On the Asiatic side, a man called Aper-el, whose name indicates his Near Eastern roots, rose to the rank of vizier (the highest civil office below that of the king himself) in the late 18th Dynasty, and there were many other Asiatics who gained powerful positions among the Egyptian elite at this date.

In 2017, a pioneering scientific project shed fresh light on the question of Egyptian physical and genetic links with sub-Saharan Africa and the Near East. Researchers from the University of Tübingen and the Max Planck Institute for the Science of Human

History in Jena successfully recovered and analysed ancient DNA from over 150 Egyptian mummies from Abusir el-Meleq, dating widely between *c.*1400 BC and AD 400. Surprisingly perhaps, their analyses, based on mitochondrial genomes from ninety individuals, suggested that modern Egyptians share more ancestry with sub-Saharan Africans than ancient Egyptians did, whereas ancient Egyptians were found to be most closely related to ancient people from the Near East. Possible causal factors for this increase in sub-Saharan ancestry in the Egyptian population during the last millennium are, first, improved mobility down the Nile; second, increased long-distance trade between sub-Saharan Africa and Egypt; and finally the trans-Saharan slave trade, which began approximately 1,300 years ago.

Viewpoints surrounding the issue of whether Egypt was fundamentally a 'black' civilization—often described as an 'Afrocentric' position—led to a lot of controversy in the 1980s and even earlier. Afrocentrism has a long history, extending at least as far back as 1827, when an editorial in *Freedom's Journal* (the first black newspaper in the USA) proposed a relationship between Africans and ancient Egyptians. A wide spectrum of Afrocentrist arguments have been advanced and largely discredited. The most influential and controversial arguments are those presented by Martin Bernal in his three-volume work *Black Athena*, published between 1987 and 2006. Bernal claimed that ancient Egypt had been widely underestimated as an important stimulus for 'Western' civilization, but both Egyptologists and Classical scholars have pointed out many flaws in his archaeological and linguistic arguments and data, including, for instance, lack of evidence for his hypothesized Egyptian colonization of the Greek islands. The Classicist Sarah Morris—writing in the 1990s when Afrocentrist controversies were at their height—argued that Bernal's work

> has bolstered, in ways not anticipated by the author, an Afrocentrist agenda which returns many debates to ground zero and demolishes decades of scrupulous research by excellent scholars.

There is no doubt, however, that some Egyptologists in the past have been guilty of racist interpretations of the Egyptians. At the most heinous end of the scale, Grafton Elliot Smith suggested in 1909 that 'the smallest infusion of Negro-blood immediately manifests itself in a dulling of initiative and a "drag" on the further development of the arts of civilisation'. It is also difficult to read the theories advanced by Flinders Petrie concerning the establishment of pharaonic Egypt by an invading Near Eastern or even European 'master-race' without being aware of his right-wing political views (he wrote a pamphlet on the dangers of socialism) and the fact that he was an enthusiastic member of the eugenics movement, which was dedicated to 'improving' human stock by 'the study of agencies under social control that may improve or impair the racial qualities of future generations' (according to its founder, the anthropologist Sir Francis Galton). Bryan Emery's espousal of invasion theories concerning early Egypt, on the other hand, was no doubt influenced more by the diffusionist ideas of Gordon Childe, but also perhaps by pre-war British colonialism in Egypt and the Sudan.

Perhaps the last word on this should be left to C. Loring Brace, writing in 1996:

> The 'race' concept did not exist in Egypt, and it is not mentioned in Herodotus, the Bible, or any of the other writings of classical antiquity. Because it has neither biological nor social justification, we should strive to see that it is eliminated from both public and private usage. Its absence will be missed by no one, and we shall all be better off without it. R.I.P.

Gender and sexuality

Questions of Egyptian identity have occupied Egyptologists for almost as long as the subject has existed, but there are some aspects of selfhood that have been less frequently addressed, probably because Egyptologists have disproportionately tended to be white European or North American male academics. The heads of the cow-goddess Bat at the top of the Narmer Palette appear to be the only female elements of the palette's decoration (and one Egyptologist, the art historian Whitney Davis, has argued that even these may actually be the heads of a bull-god). The palette, like the majority of Egyptian art and texts, is essentially a male-dominated artefact. This raises the question of what we know of women in ancient Egypt, and indeed what we know of the Egyptians' own views on gender and sexuality. Which aspects of Egyptian society were overtly or implicitly moulded by male, female, or queer concerns?

When we look at the patterning of gender in Egyptian textual and visual sources, it is almost immediately apparent that male images and concerns are much more frequent and prominent than those of women. This male skew in the data occurs in a number of different ways, some obvious and others much more subtle and insidious. As we have seen with the summary of views of Queen Hatshepsut's reign, very few women reached the office of ruler during almost three millennia of the pharaonic period. In tomb chapels, women are regularly secondary figures, since the tombs were nearly always intended primarily for their fathers, husbands, or sons. In its texts and artistic iconography Egypt was androcentric from at least the 1st Dynasty onwards. This is partly a false impression conveyed by our biased selection of data, but it was also, in some respects, how it actually was in Egyptian society, with virtually all women being excluded from administration and the writing and reading of texts (although since at least 95 per cent of men were probably also illiterate, this may be a less significant factor). Women were also frequently invisible in the world of work, with the notable exception of textile production, brewing, and baking (although men are also shown engaged in these activities). Tomb paintings and wooden funerary models regularly show women spinning and weaving, and sometimes harvesting flax in agricultural scenes, and some texts indicate that this was one of the main activities in the royal household (a fact that seems to have escaped many Victorian Orientalist painters when they were evoking scenes of 'pharaoh's harem').

In the past, Egyptologists simply took this situation for granted, making little effort to 'unpick' the roles and lifeways of women from this male-oriented documentation. In the last fifty years, however, as the numbers of female professional Egyptologists have increased, not surprisingly greater attempts have been made to read between the lines in search of evidence for women's lives and achievements. It has become apparent, for instance, that the situation changed over time, so that there were actually three phases of the pharaonic period when women were more visible in the surviving documentation: in the Old Kingdom, when they were allowed to hold some administrative posts (although only being placed in charge of groups of women); in the early 18th Dynasty, when women were more frequently featured on funerary monuments, probably reflecting their greater ability to take part in funerary rituals; and in the period from the late 20th to the early 22nd Dynasty, when they not only appeared more often in the decoration of tomb chapels but were also increasingly shown without any male relatives in attendance.

Inevitably perhaps—given Egyptologists' long-standing predisposition to the study of elite monuments—much of the early work concentrated on research into royal and privileged women such as Hetepheres (the mother of Khufu), Sobekneferu (a female ruler at the end of the 12th Dynasty), Hatshepsut, and Nefertiti. Gradually, however, greater effort has been applied to the extraction of information on women of all classes and wealth levels, and this shift of focus has been greatly assisted and encouraged by the tendency of newly favoured settlement archaeology to produce the kind of objective socio-economic evidence that at least has the potential to reveal the more female-oriented aspects of Egypt. Those parts of domestic and public life that male documents and artistic images can render invisible are sometimes considerably more obvious in the archaeological record. A note of caution, however, needs to be sounded when it comes to analysing houses for patterns of use by different genders, since it would be all too easy to make unwarranted ethnocentric assumptions concerning definitions of male and female space (e.g. women/kitchen, men/reception room, women/bedroom).

Another aspect of gender studies in which Egyptologists have often been guilty of ethnocentricity is in the area of sexuality. In Chapter 8 I discuss the fact that Egyptian religion includes an explicit focus on the phalluses of certain deities. Many Egyptologists, brought up almost entirely in the Judaeo-Christian religious traditions, have, academically speaking, averted their eyes from this phallocentrism, regarding it, consciously or subconsciously, as somehow inappropriate in a religious context. Broadly speaking, this led many scholars to attempt to downplay such episodes as the description of Atum's act of masturbation in order to create the next generation of deities (in the absence of any goddess with which to procreate).

Only two books have so far been written on sex in pharaonic and Graeco-Roman Egypt, but one characteristic Egyptological assumption that both authors highlight is the conventional tendency to assign sexually related artefacts and images to the more anodyne area of 'fertility' rather than acknowledging overtly sexual images and activities. As Lynn Meskell has put it,

> Women's sexuality, not their fertility (i.e. pregnancy) is stressed in tomb scenes, and their sexual qualities were presumably a sought after commodity in the afterlife as were provisions of servants and food.

Tom Hare, however, points out more cautiously that it may often be difficult to decide when representations are actually intended to be erotic or not:

> However attractive we may find the painting of a bare-breasted Egyptian woman or goddess, we would be rash to read into this an

erotic interest beyond our own personal interest. This is because in formal canonical representation, adult women and goddesses are often depicted bare-breasted, with the nipple of the forward breast delineated.

He goes on to discuss the complexity of the picture we are presented with, given that statues show women in particular types of dress which in this context conceal the breasts, and yet the same dresses in two-dimensional depictions may show one of the breasts—this appears to be some kind of artistic convention rather than eroticization. On the other hand, he accepts that there is almost certainly deliberate sexuality observable in the appearance, in mid-18th-Dynasty elite tombs, of fully nude female dancers, musicians, and servants (Figure 12), and therefore suggests that, in these contexts, 'the female figure is clearly the object of the male subject's gaze'.

Evidence for same-sex desire in ancient Egypt

While heterosexuality is relatively easy to find in Egyptian texts and images, the same cannot be said for same-sex relations; for this topic, there are only occasional clues and allusions, and even these are often disputed or difficult to interpret. In addition, as some researchers have pointed out, the very idea of heterosexuality and homosexuality as two distinct categories is something of a recent binary construct that we impose on the distant past at our peril. The situation is not helped by the fact that, compared with modern art and literature, ancient Egyptian sources are relatively low on overt sexual references (notwithstanding the phallocentricity of some of the religious motifs mentioned above). Sexual acts of any kind between individuals are rarely represented or discussed—a few notable artistic exceptions are the Turin Erotic Papyrus, some erotic ostraca, and a well-known sketch found in the entrance of a Middle Kingdom tomb above Hatshepsut's mortuary temple (the latter often interpreted, highly speculatively, as a scene of the

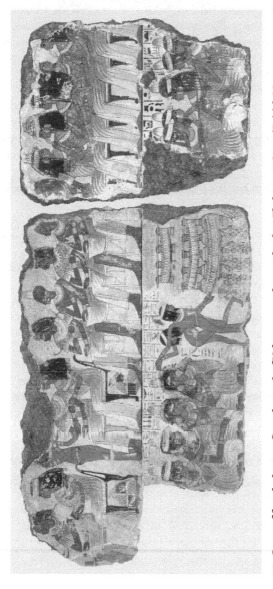

12. Scene of female dancers from the tomb of Nebamun, on the west bank at Thebes, c.1160 BC (British Museum EA37984).

queen being penetrated from behind by her official Senenmut). The main literary allusion to same-sex intercourse takes place in various versions of the myth of Horus and Seth, and involves anal sex between the young god Horus and his uncle Seth—the earliest example of this appears in the Pyramid Texts: 'Horus has insinuated his semen into the backside of Seth; Seth has insinuated his semen into the backside of Horus.' In later versions of the myth, such as the 20th-Dynasty Papyrus Chester Beatty I, the narrative seems to stress Seth's role as the sodomizer and the act seems to be very much about Seth exerting dominance over Horus. The implication is that the Egyptians at this date were neutral about homosexuality in itself but focused more on the perceived weakness of the man being penetrated.

One piece of evidence that has played a pivotal role in the search for evidence of same-sex relationships in pharaonic Egypt is a 5th-Dynasty tomb at Saqqara belonging to a pair of male royal manicurists named Niankhkhnum and Khnumhotep (*c.*2445–2421 **BC**) (Figure 13). Not only did these two individuals share a tomb, but the sculptured relief images on the walls of the funerary chapel show them embracing one another and, in one case, touching noses in a manner that can usually be taken to depict the act of kissing. Interestingly, both men appear to have had wives, but their female partners play a very minimal role in the tomb decoration (each appearing only about three or four times, whereas their husbands are portrayed around thirty times)—as Nadine Cherpion has put it: 'Let us say that... psychologically, there was no room for them in the tomb, especially in images such as those in which Niankhkhnum and Khnumhotep embrace one another.' It should of course be noted that not all researchers agree that these two individuals were lovers—a persistent alternative view is that they may have been twins (like the two men called Hor and Suty on a New Kingdom stele in the British Museum, who are said to have been born 'on the same day'), and perhaps that they may even have been

13. The two royal manicurists, Niankhkhnum and Khnumhotep, in the wall decoration of their 5th-Dynasty *mastaba*-tomb at Saqqara, c.2445–2421 BC.

conjoined twins. Scholars such as Greg Reeder have nevertheless argued strongly that the physical closeness and intimacy of Niankhkhnum and Khnumhotep, including a double statue in which they are portrayed holding hands, seem to be comparable only with images in other tombs that show heterosexual couples. In one scene, for instance, Khnumhotep is shown holding a lotus up to his nose in a manner which is almost always associated with women at this early date. A scene at the entrance to the innermost chamber of the tomb shows the two men embracing very closely in a way that almost exactly parallels the embrace between Kha-hay and his wife Meret-yetes in a nearby tomb of slightly earlier date. Despite Reeder's compelling arguments, many Egyptologists remain unconvinced that this is anything other than projection of modern views onto ancient imagery.

Ethnicity, race, gender, and sexuality in ancient Egypt are surely among the most controversial and fascinating areas of current

Egyptological research. Since the modern Western world itself is deeply immersed in identity crises, from 'ethnic cleansing' and 'race hate' to feminism and LGBT+ issues, it is hardly surprising that ancient Egyptian source material has become fresh grist to these mills.

Chapter 7
Death

The Narmer Palette and the Narmer Mace-head, two of the most significant artefacts from King Narmer's reign, were both discovered at Hierakonpolis. The burial of Narmer himself, however, has been identified at Abydos, 150 km to the north-west of Hierakonpolis. His tomb seems to have been located alongside those of the other rulers of Dynasties 0 and 1, in Cemetery B, at the site of Umm el-Qa'ab, at the western edge of Abydos.

It is in fact a slightly later 1st-Dynasty tomb at Abydos—the burial of King Djer (perhaps Narmer's grandson) that is most relevant to the subject of this chapter: the cult of Osiris and Egyptian attitudes to the dead. Djer's tomb, covering an area of 70 × 40 metres, including the subsidiary burials in rows, was the largest in the Early Dynastic royal cemetery at Abydos. It was here that Flinders Petrie found part of a linen-wrapped arm wearing precious bracelets hidden in the north wall of the tomb, and therefore saved when the tomb was burnt in ancient times. This may be the one surviving fragment of an actual royal body in the Early Dynastic cemetery as a whole, although sadly only the jewellery and a few of the linen bandages survive today (the former in the Egyptian Museum, Cairo, and the latter in the Petrie Museum, University College London), removing any real possibility of the limb being scientifically dated to establish or refute its contemporaneity with Djer.

By the Middle Kingdom, if not earlier, the tomb of Djer had been converted into a cenotaph (literally 'empty tomb') of the god Osiris, thus transforming it into a centre of 'pilgrimage' containing a stone image of the god, which was discovered still in place when the French archaeologist Émile Amélineau first excavated the burial in 1897. The tomb seems to have eventually been regarded as the ultimate, quintessential royal funerary memorial: the mythical burial place of the god Osiris, whose entire religious cult was intimately connected with the concept of the dead king. So, who or what was Osiris, and why is he so important to our understanding of death, mummies, and all the rest?

'Foremost of the westerners'

Osiris, the god of the dead and the afterlife, is one of the earliest members of the Egyptian pantheon, probably starting off as a fertility god linked with agriculture, and perhaps also the Nile 'inundation'. Like many other major deities, he gradually acquired the attributes of other gods as his worship spread throughout the country. At a fairly early stage Osiris seems to have taken over the insignia of the god Andjety, from whom he also took the mythical attribute of deity as dead ruler. Andjety's cult centre Djedu, in the Delta, therefore later became known as Busiris (meaning 'house/sanctuary of Osiris'), and was said to be the place identified with Osiris' backbone (the symbol of which was the *djed*-pillar). The combination of Osiris' associations with fertility and death almost inevitably ensured that he became the ultimate god of resurrection, and the link with the dead king was established by the 5th Dynasty at the latest. It became essential for the mummified body to be associated with Osiris in order to gain eternal life (Figure 14).

Ancient Egyptian texts have a tendency to allude to various divine myths through references to rituals and the use of various epithets, but their literature is notoriously lacking in straightforward narrative-style myths. Reconstructing Egyptian

14. Image of the god Osiris in the 19th-Dynasty tomb of Sennedjem at Deir el-Medina, western Thebes, *c*.1280 BC.

mythology from ancient Egyptian texts can be rather like piecing together the biblical account of the birth of Jesus from a series of Christmas cards and carols. Consequently, the myths associated with Osiris are best known not from an Egyptian source but from a much later compilation of the legend by the Greek writer Plutarch (AD *c*.46–126). Some elements of Plutarch's version have been corroborated by surviving fragments of the stories in Egyptian sources, but others may possibly be Greek or Roman inventions. He describes Osiris as a human ruler whose accidental(!) adultery with his sister-in-law Nephthys caused his evil brother Seth to become jealous and to plot secretly against him. Seth discovered the measurements of his brother's body and had a magnificent casket made to fit him. He next organized a banquet to which he invited seventy-two accomplices as well as Osiris. During the feast he brought forward the chest and declared that whoever fitted it exactly should have it as a gift. Having stepped into the coffin, Osiris was locked inside, and the lid was sealed with molten lead. The coffin was then thrown into the Nile and eventually drifted down to the Mediterranean, washing up at the Syrian port of Byblos. This city always had strong links with ancient Egypt, particularly through the supply of cedar-wood, therefore it is perhaps no surprise that the coffin is then said to have become entangled in a cedar tree.

Osiris's wife Isis eventually rescues him and returns to Egypt, hiding him in his coffin in the marshes prior to giving him a decent burial. However, Seth is said to have stumbled on the casket and angrily dismembered the body of his brother, scattering the body-parts (their number varies in different accounts, from 14 to 42) throughout Egypt. Isis searches for the body-parts and buries each at the place where it is found. Plutarch's version of the story claims that the phallus was eaten by the Nile carp (*Lepidotus*), the *Phagrus*, and the *Oxyrynchus* fish, so that an artificial penis had to be manufactured, but it is noticeable that none of the fragmentary Egyptian accounts suggests this, since the fertile phallus was a crucial element in the cult. The original Egyptian versions also add another episode after Osiris's dismembered body was reassembled into the form of the first mummy—they describe how Isis was impregnated by the mummified body, and conceived the child Horus. This moment of conception is sometimes portrayed in a scene showing Isis in the form of a kite hovering on the mummy's penis. Versions of the scene have been found both in the shrine of Sokar–Osiris in the temple of Seti I at Abydos and also in one of the roof chambers of the temple of Hathor at Dendera.

Many of the principal features of the myth of Osiris and Isis are already attested by the Old Kingdom (2686–2160), including his death by drowning, and the discovery of his body by Isis. The identification of Seth, the god of the desert and chaos, as his murderer was in place by the Middle Kingdom (2040–1640), although the story doesn't yet explicitly refer to his dismemberment of the dead Osiris. It is the process of dismemberment, however, that provides the most telling insights into Egyptian culture. We can rarely be sure whether myths reflect ritual or inspire it, or whether other kinds of processes lie behind the surviving texts and images, but there seems to be a web of links between the myth of Osiris and the process of mummification. Herodotus' very detailed account of Egyptian mummification describes the main practitioners as *paraschistai* ('slitters') and *taricheutai* ('picklers'), and, although the terms are somewhat irreverent, they give a good sense of the two principal stages: the body must first be cut up and to some extent dismembered by the slitters before it can be reassembled and preserved by the picklers. The Osiris myth is therefore a very accurate prototype for the practical process of physical preservation (and of course the reverse may be true—that the myth emerged as a way of providing divine precedent for the mummification process).

Although the cult of Osiris permeates Egyptian funerary beliefs in various forms, there are probably two particular aspects of the cult that are most prominent and influential. The first of these is the way in which, by the New Kingdom, it became increasingly common for funerary texts to make explicit connections between the deceased and Osiris, and for the descriptions of the fate of any dead individual to deliberately echo parts of the myth. The second is the significance of the site of Abydos as a focus for private funerary cults. The survival of large numbers of private funerary stelae and cenotaphs dedicated at Abydos by a whole variety of individuals shows that the cult of Osiris became extremely popular (in the literal sense of the word) from at least as early as the end of the Old Kingdom. Even when individuals were unable to place stelae or monuments at Abydos itself, they incorporated items or images in their tombs that refer to the act of making a pilgrimage to Abydos. The idea of the imaginary journey to Abydos (described by Egyptians as a 'voyage in peace') first appeared in the Middle Kingdom in the tombs of the local governors Amenemhat and Khnumhotep II, taking the form of painted scenes showing boats sailing to and from the cult-place, while the texts describe the deceased man's participation in the festival of Osiris. Many Middle Kingdom tombs also contained model boats symbolizing the voyage of the body of the deceased to and from the home of Osiris.

By the late Middle Kingdom, the creation of private funerary monuments at Abydos had evidently already become so prevalent that the 13th-Dynasty ruler Wegaf issued a decree forbidding tombs to be built on the processional way. The apparent expansion of Osirid funerary privileges beyond the immediate sphere of the royal family was once famously (and rather inaccurately) described by the American Egyptologist John Wilson as the 'democratization of the afterlife'. Wilson, and many later Egyptologists, argued that, from the Middle Kingdom onwards, once-royal funerary privileges were gradually extended to ordinary people, allowing them to physically take part in the rites of Osiris and thus acquire funerary benefits that had previously been restricted to kings. Although many popular books (and even textbooks) on Egypt still express this view, few researchers now feel that the paradigm of 'democratization' can seriously be applied to the gradual spread of funerary rites across Egyptian society. As Mark Smith puts it:

> There is no compelling reason to assume that a king's expectations with regard to the next world would have differed greatly from those of an ordinary person, or that the rites performed to ensure his posthumous well-being would have taken a form radically different from theirs. Nor is there any basis for the widespread assumption that any innovations in this area must have had their origin in the royal sphere prior to being adopted by non-royal individuals...With some changes, the reverse may have been true.

In other words, Egyptian mummification and funerary rites should no longer be regarded as primarily royal in origin or nature, not least because the evidence (and the dating) can often be so patchy that we cannot really say with full certainty at which points in time different members of Egyptian society adopted particular strategies in relation to death and the afterlife.

Ancient Egyptian attitudes to death

Another old cliché—the idea that Egyptians were totally obsessed with death—is in danger of being eclipsed by a new cliché, since many recent books have made the point that Egyptian tombs contain ample evidence that they were actually obsessed with *life*, in the form of endless 'daily life' scenes and models, depicting individuals working in the fields, making wine, banqueting, playing music, dancing, and numerous other life-affirming activities. In reality, if we are going to caricature the Egyptians, there are good grounds for assuming that their real concerns—as in many other cultures—lay somewhere between these two extremes. Certainly in the elite sphere of society they devoted more of their time and financial resources to preparations for death than we would necessarily consider healthy. However, it is equally certain that our view of their society has always been disproportionately biased towards the funerary side of things, partly because cemeteries and other funerary phenomena were invariably placed in the desert and have therefore been much better preserved than their houses, towns, and marketplaces. Settlements were typically located in wetter conditions closer to the Nile or other sources of water, and they have also tended to be covered by modern towns and cities, which naturally gravitate towards wetter, more fertile locations. The fact that so much of our excavated evidence relates to death and the afterlife is also a direct result of many Egyptologists' own preference for specialization in these topics. Until recently many research agendas were geared towards funerary or religious matters rather than social or economic trends, although this situation has changed significantly in recent decades, with more research projects focusing on the survey and excavation of towns and cities.

Nevertheless, the vast majority of Egyptological evidence is still oriented more towards death than life.

The ancient Egyptians' attitudes to life and death were heavily influenced by their steadfast belief that eternal life could be ensured by a wide range of strategies, including piety to the gods, the preservation of the body through mummification, and the provision of statuary and other funerary equipment. The survival of numerous tombs and funerary texts has enabled Egyptologists to explore the complexity and gradual elaboration of this belief system. Each human individual was considered to comprise not only a physical body but also three other crucial elements, known as the *ka*, *ba*, and *akh*, all of which were regarded as essential to human survival both before and after death. Each person's name and shadow were also considered to be living entities, crucial to human existence, rather than simply linguistic and natural phenomena. The essence of each individual was contained in the sum of all these parts, none of which could be neglected.

This consciousness of individuals as composites of various types of identity brings us back again to the theme of dismemberment (and reassembling), which was discussed above in relation to the cult of Osiris. One of the reasons that such themes feature so prominently in Egyptian attitudes to death is because the act of ensuring any individual's enjoyment of the afterlife was a delicate business of separation and assembly. All of these separate elements (the body, *ka*, *ba*, *akh*, shadow, and name) had to be sustained and protected from harm. At the most basic level this could be achieved by burying the body with a set of funerary equipment, and in its most elaborate form the royal cult could include a number of temples complete with priests and a steady flow of offerings, usually financed by gifts of agricultural land and other economic resources. A wide diversity of surviving funerary texts (the Pyramid Texts, Coffin Texts, and various Books of the Netherworld) present a set of descriptions of the afterlife that often conflict with one another. One scenario, for instance, envisages the transformation of humans into circumpolar stars, while another proposes the continuation of normal life in an afterworld sometimes described as the Field of Reeds.

Ancient, modern, and postmodern mummies

Until recently it was assumed that the earliest *artificial* mummies (as opposed to bodies simply desiccated by the surrounding sand) were those found at cemeteries such as Abydos, Saqqara, and Tarkhan in the Early Dynastic period. However, in 1997 a team of archaeologists led by Renée Friedman working in one of the non-elite Predynastic cemeteries at Hierakonpolis found three intact burials containing female bodies with their heads, necks, and hands wrapped in linen bandages, the whole of each of the corpses being swathed in linen and matting. The grave goods accompanying these bodies dated to around 3600 BC (the early Naqada II culture), therefore pushing back the earliest use of artificial mummification to a much earlier period than previously supposed, although opinions differ as to whether the simple bandaging of parts of a corpse can necessarily be described as mummification. Intriguingly, one of the women had her throat cut after death, suggesting that even at this date there might have been a sense in which the ritual dismemberment and reassembly of Osiris's body-parts was being acted out.

This is not the end of the story, however—the work of an Anglo-Australian team of scientists led by Egyptologist Jana Jones has demonstrated that the use of mummification techniques can be pushed back even further in time to the Neolithic period. Jones examined linen wrappings from bodies in securely provenanced pit graves in the earliest recorded ancient Egyptian cemeteries at Mostagedda, in the Badari region of Upper Egypt, using a combination of gas chromatography-mass spectrometry (GC-MS) and thermal desorption/pyrolysis (TD/Py)-GC-MS. These analyses resulted in the identification of a number of organic substances such as pine resin, an aromatic plant extract, a plant gum/sugar, a natural petroleum source, and a plant oil/animal fat in the wrappings, which have been radiocarbon-dated to *c*.4300–3800 BC. The earliest of these wrappings therefore contain embalming materials evidently made from complex recipes using the same kind of ingredients, in roughly the same proportions, as embalmed wrappings used in early pharaonic mummification some 1500 years later. Jones and her team have argued that the kinds of materials being used by Neolithic embalmers already show an awareness of the antibacterial properties of some of these substances, and clearly already managed to achieve localized soft-tissue preservation.

Some early pharaonic forms of Egyptian mummification seem to have evolved simply to preserve the image of the body—thus some of the early mummies of the 3rd millennium BC were simply painted with plaster and paint, preserving the outer shell of the body but allowing the flesh to decay away inside. The development of more sophisticated techniques meant that gradually more of the original body was retained, eventually reaching something of a peak in the late New Kingdom and Third Intermediate Period (*c*.1200–900 BC). By the time Herodotus wrote his detailed description of the process of mummification, around the middle of the 5th century BC, techniques are thought to have already gone into something of a decline, presumably partly in order to meet the demands of 'mass production' as mummification spread through larger numbers of the population. In 2018, a Late Period embalming workshop, dating to *c*.600–400 BC, was excavated at Saqqara by an Egypto-German archaeological team, revealing a good range of the kind of equipment that would have been used to mummify human and animal bodies at around the time of Herodotus. An open area of the workshop incorporates two large basins that may once have held natron, a type of salt used to desiccate corpses. The finds also include numerous measuring cups bearing hieratic and demotic labels and instructions—these are thought to have contained various oils for use in embalming—once their residual contents have been analysed, it may be possible to deduce the terminology and recipes relating to some of the key embalming ingredients in use at this date.

The preservation of the body by mummification was an essential part of ancient Egyptian funerary practice, since it was to the body that the *ka*, or double, would return in order to find sustenance. If the body had disintegrated or become unrecognizable the *ka* would not be able to feed and the chances of reaching the afterlife would diminish.

My own first encounter with the concept of the Egyptian *ka* came in the form of a Dennis Wheatley novel: *The Ka of Gifford Hillary*, published in 1956, which must have played a small part in enticing me towards the study of Egypt. I now know that the eponymous ghost-like phenomenon in the novel (who manages to float around solving his own murder, like the central character in the 1980s movie *Ghost*) is probably more of a *ba* than a *ka* (see the glossary for the differences between the two), but considering the many much greater crimes committed against Egyptology by modern books and films, it would be a little churlish to pick on Wheatley, who had at least done a little serious research.

Mummies (and their resuscitation) have a very long literary and cinematic history, stretching back at least as far as 1827, when Jane Webb Loudon published *The Mummy—A Tale of the 22nd Century*, in which the body of Cheops, builder of the Great Pyramid, is resurrected. This book essentially belonged to the Gothic fiction genre, like Mary Shelley's slightly earlier *Frankenstein*. Later novelists whose fiction pioneered the whole mummy genre include many whose names we would expect: Théophile Gautier (*The Mummy's Foot*, 1840), Edgar Allan Poe (*Some Words with a Mummy*, 1845), H. H. Rider Haggard (*She*, 1887; *Smith and the Pharaohs*, 1912–13), Sir Arthur Conan Doyle (*The Ring of Thoth*, 1890; *Lot No. 249*, 1892), Bram Stoker (*The Jewel of Seven Stars*, 1903), and Sax Rohmer (*She Who Sleeps*, 1928, and many others). One intriguing theory put forward by

Nicholas Daly is that the spate of late Victorian and Edwardian mummy tales was inspired by the changing nature of the British Empire, with the mummies subconsciously representing the dangerous and exotic materials pursued by empire-builders.

The first cinematic rendition of a resuscitated and vengeful mummy seems to have been *Cléopâtre*, a one-minute-long silent movie made by Georges Méliès in 1899, but the best-known feature-length film of this type is undoubtedly *The Mummy*, directed by Karl Freund in 1932 and starring Boris Karloff as Imhotep. In Freund's film, the body of Imhotep is revived by archaeologists reading from a 'scroll of Thoth'. This plot actually draws on a rare example of an ancient Egyptian tale of a revived body, the cycle of Setne Khaemwaset, written in the demotic script on papyri dating to the Ptolemaic and Roman periods. However, the principal literary source for the film seems to have been Nina Wilcox Putnam's *Cagliostro*. Rider Haggard's *She* (the film version of which was written by John Balderston, who had also scripted *The Mummy*) and Conan Doyle's *The Ring of Thoth* were both also possible influences. Since the 1930s, there have been numerous other mummy movies, in fact enough to have established this as very much a genre in its own right. Probably best not even to discuss Alex Kurtzman's 2017 remake of *The Mummy*, for which Tom Cruise received a 'golden raspberry' as worst actor, and Kurtzman was nominated as worst director.

The curse…

In discussing mummies, we can hardly ignore the continual association in literature and films, particularly in the 20th century, between mummies and dreadful curses, usually affecting the archaeologist who has disturbed an Egyptian corpse's rest. Where did this all start, and more importantly is there any truth in it? One answer to the second part of the question is that, if these curses genuinely existed, then I and several of my Egyptological colleagues would surely have long ago succumbed to the kind of mosquito-infected cut that polished off Lord Carnarvon shortly after the opening of Tutankhamun's tomb. As for where it all started, there were certainly ancient Egyptian funerary inscriptions that included threats against those who might damage or neglect the tomb in some way, so there is very early evidence of a kind. However, if we want to find someone to blame for promoting the idea that such curses actually worked, then the name that springs immediately to mind is the Egyptologist Arthur Weigall, who was reporting as a journalist for the *Daily Mail* during the first few weeks of the removal of funerary equipment from Tutankhamun's tomb. As if the discovery in itself was not sufficiently exciting, Weigall seems to have hit upon the idea of mentioning the curse (although claiming not to believe in it himself) as a way of spicing up his dispatches. The first novelist to use the mummy's curse as part of a narrative was probably Louisa May Alcott, the writer of *Little Women*, who published a story called *Lost in a Pyramid; or the Mummy's Curse* in 1869, so Weigall would have been able to draw on a good fifty years of fictional material on this theme.

Chapter 8
Religion

The pairs of cow's heads with huge curling horns depicted at the top of the Narmer Palette are part of the imagery of an early cow-goddess named Bat, who was patroness of the seventh nome (province) of Upper Egypt. She is a rather poorly known deity, partly because, by the Middle Kingdom, her cult had been absorbed into that of another much more prominent cow-goddess, Hathor. Unlike Hathor, who might be represented as a cow or cow-headed woman, Bat was portrayed (on the rare occasions that she appears in Egyptian art) with a body in the shape of the sistrum (a rattle-like musical instrument characteristically played by women). The body is not visible on the Narmer Palette, but Bat is described in the Pyramid Texts as 'with her two faces', which would tie in with her double representation on either side of the palette. Throughout the history of Egyptian religion the cults of minor deities were continually being absorbed into those whose worship was more widespread or more favoured by the kings of that time.

As Erik Hornung, one of the most influential researchers into Egyptian religion, has pointed out, 'In their constantly changing nature and manifestations, the Egyptian gods resemble the country's temples, which were never finished and complete, but always "under construction".' Hornung also argues that there was probably a form of monotheism underlying the superficially polytheistic Egyptian religion for much of the pharaonic period.

The cow's heads of Bat are an appropriate starting point for a consideration of Egyptologists' views on ancient Egyptian religion, given that images of hybrid animal-headed or bird-headed deities are usually the first ones that come to mind. It is noticeable also that these elaborate deities made up of human and bestial body-parts appear to interact directly with at least some of the human population of Egypt. One of the most important differences between our world-view and that of the Egyptians lies in the field of metaphysics. We make a clear distinction between the natural and supernatural worlds (as part of our inheritance of Greek philosophical thought) whereas the Egyptians saw both deities and humans as interacting on the same social and physical planes.

If ancient Egyptian culture as a whole is often difficult to comprehend, then Egyptian religion is among the most problematic topics that Egyptologists have been obliged to tackle. A great deal of surviving Egyptian art is connected with religion, but usually it is much easier to describe and to categorize than to analyse or interpret effectively. The many questions that Egyptologists have had difficulties in answering conclusively include the following. Did Egyptians actually imagine their deities to exist in the 'real world' as hybrids of human and non-human characteristics, from the surprisingly plausible rendition of the god Horus as a falcon-headed man to the rather less convincing (to our eyes) representation of the sun-god Khepri as a man whose head is entirely replaced by a scarab beetle? Or did they simply create these images as elaborate symbols and metaphors representing the characteristics or personalities of their deities? When we are shown a jackal-headed figure embalming the body of the deceased are we supposed to believe that Anubis, the god of the underworld, was actually responsible for all mummifications or are we being shown a priest-embalmer wearing a mask allowing him to impersonate the god (and if so was he then regarded as actually becoming the god or simply imitating him during the ritual)? There is one surviving full-size pottery mask in the form of Anubis's jackal head (now in the Pelizaeus Museum, Hildesheim) but this does not really solve the above series of problems. Part of the urgency with which Egyptologists tend to attack such questions probably derives from our desire to find out whether the systems of thought of ancient Egypt were fundamentally different from our own, or whether they just appear so because they are expressed in ways that are now very difficult to interpret.

When most scholars write about Egyptian religion they focus principally on the archaeological remains of what appear to be sacred structures, and on the textual and iconographic clues to theological thought. Barry Kemp makes the point that most of our knowledge of Egyptian 'temple religion' is concerned with the symbolism and ritual of the large state temples, whereas we still know relatively little about the ways in which such buildings were used by people, whether priests, scribes, or normal members of the population. The masses were evidently rarely allowed to penetrate beyond the temples' outer courtyards, relying on festivals, when deities' images were sometimes carried from one shrine to another. These were the rare moments when 'normal' Egyptians were able to gain any physical interaction with the cult images. For many Egyptologists, this has led to the assertion that Egyptian religion was founded on the concepts of secrecy and revelation, both of which were bolstered and elaborated through myth, ritual, and temple architecture. It was in the course of rituals, festivals, and dramas that the divine reality seems to have been constantly acted out or actualized. Ritual and regular celebration of festivals were ways of repeatedly reinforcing the links between myth and reality. Each temple was therefore not simply the 'home' of one or more deities but a set of rooms connected with the performance of rituals and festivals. In a sense the temples simply served as a means of channelling and recording the movements of offerings and divine images in and out of the various shrines.

Religious origins

The history of Egyptian religion was at one stage concerned principally with the beliefs and temples of the pharaonic period. Now it has become increasingly clear that, as with the rest of Egyptian culture, there is a significant prehistory of Egyptian religion that needs to be documented and analysed if the later material is to be properly understood. At the Neolithic site of Nabta Playa (in the Western Desert, *c.*100 km west of Abu Simbel), for instance, circular and linear arrangements of small standing stones were identified in 1992 (and later moved to the Nubian Museum, Aswan, in 2008, to protect them from vandalism). These alignments of stones indicated that monuments oriented to astronomical phenomena—the cardinal points and the summer solstice—were already being created as early as 4000 BC. Alongside one of the alignments were found two tumuli covering burials of long-horned bulls, while further cattle burials, surmounted by large stones, were discovered in one of the wadis leading into the Nabta Playa depression. All of this strongly suggests that some form of cow/bull cult already existed among the cattle-herding people of the Egyptian deserts in the early 4th millennium BC, evidently prefiguring both the emergence of such cow-goddesses as Bat and Hathor and the very strong associations between Egyptian kings and bulls. Comparisons between female figures in early prehistoric petroglyphs, Predynastic female figurines (Figure 15), and some of the religious motifs of the pharaonic period appear to show a high degree of continuity in the iconography, although it would be simplistic to assume that the use of similar icons or artistic themes is necessarily an indication of long-term connections in the underlying religious beliefs.

15. Predynastic painted clay figurine representing a woman (or goddess?) with upraised arms, from el-Ma'mariya, Naqada IIa period, *c.*3600 BC (Brooklyn Museum 07.447.505).

In 1985–9, archaeology provided one intriguing insight into the crucial phase of religious development towards the end of Egyptian prehistory. Excavations in a section of the Predynastic town at Hierakonpolis (Locality HK29A) revealed a large area interpreted as an early religious complex, probably incorporating a parabolic courtyard, a colossal divine image of some kind, a ceremonial gateway, and four large post-holes, which may show the location of a monumental façade, all dating to Naqada IIB–IIIA (*c.*3600–3350). As with the Nabta Playa remains, there were copious traces of butchery and feasting in association with this early ritual structure. Acts of animal sacrifice and the piling up of offerings to the gods seem to have been crucial elements of the early religion of Egypt, and in later times they still dominate Egyptian worship. Fresh excavations at HK29A in 2002 and 2008 revealed a large wooden palisade wall suggesting that the complex was only one part of a monumental compound potentially covering an area of over a hectare. More recent work at Hierakonpolis has also revealed that other large wood-columned structures—associated with elite burials and therefore perhaps intended for enactment of funerary rites—were built at around the same time as the HK29A ritual area. Similar early wooden-pillared ritual structures were excavated at the sites of Mahasna and Naqada in the early 2000s, suggesting that Hierakonpolis HK29A was not an isolated instance of early temple architecture.

These strong early associations between temple courtyards and the provision of offerings and sacrifices continue to dominate much of the pictorial and textual decoration of later Egyptian temples. Many of the texts inscribed on the walls of temples throughout the pharaonic and Graeco-Roman periods are connected with the listing of the nature and quantity of offerings delivered to the gods' shrines. For instance, the walls of Medinet Habu, the mortuary temple of Ramesses III, are decorated with seventy-one offerings, the largest surviving set of offering lists in any of the New Kingdom royal mortuary temples. The most frequent kind of offering was bread (indeed the hieroglyph meaning 'offering' was a depiction of a loaf on a mat), with lists of more than 5,500 loaves and 204 jars of beer being offered every day. The loaves were of several different types, the most common being round *pesen* and tapering cylindrical moulded *bit*. This is one of the rare occasions where a fruitful connection can be made between the textual and archaeological sides of ancient Egypt, since sherds from the cylindrical *bit* bread-moulds have been found in abundance at Medinet Habu and other religious sites; these *bit* loaves seem to have been more closely associated with religious festivals than standard forms of bread.

If the provision of offerings represents a relatively familiar aspect of Egyptian religion for the modern Western observer, there is another recurrent aspect of many of the religious cults that Egyptologists of the late 19th and early 20th century frequently preferred to ignore (or at least gloss over). This was the tendency towards 'phallocentrism', involving cults dedicated to very obviously ithyphallic gods (especially Min and Amun). Although Egyptian art shied away from depicting the sexual act, it had no such qualms about the depiction of the erect phallus. Indeed, as Tom Hare points out, 'a celebration of the phallus is one of the central iconic foci of Egyptian religion from predynastic days through the Roman occupation'. The three oldest colossal religious statues in Egyptian history, found by Petrie in the earliest strata of the temple of Min at Koptos (and now in the Ashmolean Museum, Oxford and the Egyptian Museum, Cairo), were essentially large ithyphallic representations, probably representing the fertility god Min. The dating of these statues has proved to be difficult and controversial but they are thought to be no later than *c.*3100 BC, the time of Narmer. This celebration of the phallus appears to be directly related to the Egyptians' concerns with the creation (and sustaining) of the universe, in which the king was thought to play a significant role—which was no doubt one of the reasons why the Egyptian state would have been concerned to ensure that the ithyphallic figures continued to be important elements of many cults.

Egyptian religion and kingship

Such is the king's domination of the evidence for religion in the pharaonic period that some Egyptologists have suggested that virtually all Egyptian state-controlled religious cults are in some sense also designed to focus attention on the royal person. This situation is probably best expressed by the one phrase that suffuses a great deal of Egyptian religious practice: the so-called 'offering formula'. This phrase occurs at the beginning of lists of types of offerings and consists of the words *hetep di nesw* ('an offering that the king gives'). In other words, each individual's acts of worship and offering to deities were circumscribed by his or her links to the king. The falcon-god Horus is one of the most prominent images on the front of the Narmer Palette, suggesting that the king, who was very much identified with Horus, was already playing a central role in the celebration of religious cults and worship in the 1st Dynasty.

It might also be argued that part of the overall purpose of the Narmer Palette was to serve as a kind of elaborate reference to the king's role in the act of providing the gods with offerings, which might consist of anything from fruit to slaughtered enemies or prisoners of war. There are a number of constantly repeated iconographic themes in the palette's decoration: first, the king smiting a foreigner, second, the siege and capture of settlements, third, the binding up of prisoners and their execution, and fourth, the offering of the spoils of war to the Egyptian gods. These acts can all be encompassed within a very simple theme in which the role of the Egyptian king was to fight battles on behalf of the gods and then bring back the prisoners and booty to dedicate to the gods in their temples. In much later periods, royal military campaigns in Nubia and Syria–Palestine are portrayed on temple walls with a very similar sequence of episodes.

Religion and ideology

A crucial distinction needs to be made between the above discussion of the emergence and development of cults, shrines, and temples, and, on the other hand, the surviving records of Egyptian ideology and codes of social behaviour. The owners of tomb-chapels in the Old Kingdom seem to have already felt a need to assert their moral right to the monument that was ensuring their enjoyment of the afterlife. Each of them would therefore claim that the tomb had been built on new ground, and that the craftsmen had been paid, and so on. Gradually, however, these more pragmatic down-to-earth statements were supplemented by moral assertions. The accepted code of social behaviour and the distinction between right and wrong during the pharaonic period both tend to be closely intertwined with funerary beliefs and cultic requirements. The earliest indications of Egyptian philosophical and ethical ideas can therefore be found embedded in funerary texts. These at first took the form of various statements included along with the offering formula, particularly on the so-called 'false-door stele', and later as elements in texts conventionally described as the 'autobiographies' of individuals, such as those of Harkhuf (at Aswan) or Ankhtifi (at Moalla), in which the deceased typically listed his or her good works. Ankhtifi, one of the few elite individuals whose life-story has survived from the First Intermediate Period, says:

> I am an honest man who has no equal, a man who can talk freely when others are obliged to be silent... The whole of Upper Egypt died from hunger and each individual had reached such a state of hunger that he ate his own children. But I refused to see anyone die of hunger in this province. I arranged for grain to be loaned to Upper Egypt and gave to the north grain from Upper Egypt. And I do not think that anything like this has been done by the provincial governors who came before me...

Ankhtifi is undoubtedly keen to establish links between his achievements as a local ruler and his moral authority. These funerary texts tend to be primarily concerned with justifying and vindicating the acts of individuals within an ethical context.

A number of practical statements of Egyptian ethics have survived in the form of the *sebayt* (literally 'teachings/instructions'), each comprising a series of maxims on the 'way of living truly', which were mainly written on papyrus and date from the Old Kingdom to the Roman period (*c.*2500 BC–AD 325). The oldest surviving examples of these documents describe the qualities required of a man in order to ensure success both in his lifetime and in the afterlife. Individuals were expected to satisfy their superiors and to protect those who were poorer. The earliest known *sebayt* is the text said to have been composed by the 4th-Dynasty sage Hardjedef (*c*.2525 BC), while another such document was attributed to Ptahhotep, a vizier of the 5th-Dynasty ruler Djedkara Isesi. It is likely that few of these instructions were written by their purported authors, and many, including that of Hardjedef, were almost certainly composed much later than they claim. The instructions retained their popularity throughout the pharaonic period, two of them being attributed to kings.

From the 2nd millennium BC onwards, however, the code of ethics described in the *sebayt* was less worldly, tending to measure virtue more through piety to the gods than through material success. The two most important surviving instructions from the Graeco-Roman period are the *Sayings of Ankhsheshonqy* (BM EA 10508) and the maxims recorded on Papyrus Insinger (Rijksmuseum, Leiden), which were both written in the demotic script, consisting of much shorter aphorisms compared with the *sebayt* of the pharaonic period.

Central both to Egyptian ethics and to their religious thought was the concept of *maat* (a term often translated as 'truth' or 'harmony'), which harked back to the original state of tranquillity at the moment of the creation of the universe. Hornung argued that Egyptian religion was among the first attempts to answer universal questions:

> Along with the Sumerians, the Egyptians deliver our earliest—though by no means primitive—evidence of human thought…As far back as the third millennium B.C., the Egyptians were concerned with questions that return in later European philosophy and that remain unanswered even today—questions about being and nonbeing, about the meaning of death, about the nature of cosmos and man, about the essence of time, about the basis of human society and the legitimation of power.

Chapter 9
Egyptomania

The Narmer Palette was initially interpreted as a historical document recording a number of military successes over foreigners or Lower Egyptians by means of which the first unification of the Egyptian state was achieved (see Chapter 3). More recently, however, it has been suggested that the relief decoration simply depicts a number of rituals (probably relating to the kingship) enacted in the year that this palette was brought as an offering to the temple or chapel. Egyptologists have interpreted many other aspects of the ceremonial palettes and mace-heads in a variety of ways. Just as the Narmer Palette was frequently given a very literal narrative interpretation, so the Narmer Mace-head was once widely regarded as a memorial of the king's marriage to a 'northern princess'. This theory relied primarily on the assumption that a depiction of a beardless figure in a carrying-chair was a representation of the royal bride, but it has been pointed out that the seated figure might be the image of a deity, and not even necessarily a female one. Theories such as these are good instances of the ways in which Egyptologists analyse and interpret their raw data, often producing images of the past that subconsciously reflect their own contemporary social or political contexts.

Egyptology has been heading rapidly in numerous different directions for some time, and it is currently impossible to predict which of these will ultimately be the more fruitful, exciting, or problematic. One thing that can hardly be ignored, however, is the fact that ancient Egypt is no longer simply the relatively obscure object of academic research—it is very much out there in the public domain, and there are any number of 'alternative Egypts' which, for better or worse, sit alongside what we might like to regard as the 'authentic' original. The players in this process of reinventing Egypt for different audiences and purposes range from journalists and artists to film producers, musicians, advertising executives, 'pyramidiots', and of course university lecturers and museum curators. In this recycling and exploitation of the ancient Egyptian database, some aspects of the culture and history have tended to appeal more to different ages or audiences. The growing dichotomy between the serious study of Egypt and its popularization was recognized as early as 1864 by Auguste Mariette, commenting on the first Egyptian Museum of Antiquities, which he had himself created only a year earlier:

Certainly, as an archaeologist, I would be inclined to blame these useless displays that do not do science any good; but if the Museum thus presented appeals to those for whom it is designed, if they come back often and in so doing get inoculated with a taste for the study and, I was going to say, the love of Egyptian antiquities, then I will have achieved my goal.

The modern non-Egyptological view of ancient Egypt is a dense patchwork built up of mummy mysteries, Hollywood epics, New Age pseudo-scientific blockbusters, tacky tourist souvenirs, and also a few enduring icons—human faces and artefacts that have been plucked out of their original ancient context and left to float in a postmodern vacuum, at the whim of the observer. In this chapter, I would like to examine the phenomenon of Egyptomania, whereby the flotsam and jetsam of ancient Egypt have somehow been washed up in the early 21st century, ending up in unexpected heaps scattered across our modern cultural landscape.

Interpretation in Egyptology: the case of pyramidology

One of the most obvious topics of fierce interpretative debate over the years has been the question of why the pyramids took the form that they did, and what this suggests about the purpose that they served. This 'pyramidology' is virtually a subject in its own right. Attention has focused not only on the shape but also on the precise size and spatial disposition of pyramids, as well as the detailed internal arrangement of the chambers, and the meanings of the texts inscribed on some of the internal walls. It almost goes without saying that many of the theories advanced have been among the least plausible or logical in the history of Egyptology, owing to the well-known effect that pyramids seem to exert on the mental faculties of some researchers and enthusiasts. Not surprisingly, the choice of explanations at different points in time can tell us as much about the researchers as the problem.

A useful starting point is the very commonsense explanation that the pyramidal shape is the most structurally sound way of building as high a monument as possible, with the most efficient use of building resources and greatest likelihood of long-term stability. For many people this has the disadvantage of ignoring the possibility of both (*a*) the colonization of earth by aliens from outer space and (*b*) the existence of a previously unsuspected civilization that already flourished thousands of years before the conventional emergence of ancient Egypt. It was also once seriously suggested to me that the pyramids had not been built but that they had been created by quarrying away all the surrounding stone—this doesn't actually explain their shape, but is a good example of the apparently inexhaustible thirst for explanations of pyramids that are imaginative rather than logical.

A very long-lasting myth about the pyramids connects them with the biblical story of Joseph—as early as the 5th century AD, the

Roman writer Julius Honorius suggested that they were Joseph's granaries. In 1859 John Taylor put forward the theory that the Great Pyramid was built by non-Egyptian invaders acting under God's guidance. Arab writers in the Middle Ages had a theory that the Pyramids were built at the time of Noah's flood in order to act as repositories of Egyptian wisdom and scientific knowledge. The one thing that all of these suggestions have in common is their assumption that the pyramids were in some way linked with the role played by Egypt in the Bible, since many of the early scholars studying Egypt were theologically motivated (see Chapter 1).

The great Victorian enthusiast Charles Piazzi Smyth, Astronomer Royal of Scotland and Professor of Astronomy at Edinburgh University, managed to combine both biblical and astronomical approaches in his pyramid research. Heavily influenced by the theories of the aforementioned John Taylor (who argued that the measurements of the pyramid amounted to a kind of slide-rule record of the proportions of the world as a whole), Piazzi Smyth surveyed at Giza in 1865 and declared that the Great Pyramid had been built at just the correct size in 'pyramid inches' to exactly encapsulate the circumference of earth, which, according to Taylor, the Egyptians were able to calculate through their knowledge of ℗. Piazzi Smyth then argued, in his three-volume *Life and Work at the Great Pyramid* (published in 1867), that the pyramid inch was also the unit of measurement used by the builders of Noah's Ark and Moses' tabernacle. Since the pyramid inch was conveniently virtually the same as the British inch, it was only a small step further to suggest that all this identified the British as the lost tribe of Israel, which neatly adds rampant Victorian imperialism to Piazzi Smyth's bundle of influences in his ruminations on pyramids.

Among the more recent discussions of pyramid form and purpose are those that emphasize the undoubted astronomical links of the pyramids. It has long been suggested that the so-called 'air vents' in the Great Pyramid served some astronomical function, since they are evidently carefully aligned with various stars, including the constellation of Orion (known to the Egyptians as Sah), which might have been the intended destination of the king's *ba*, when he ascended to take his place among the circumpolar stars. Kate Spence has suggested that the architects of the pyramids may have aligned their sides with the cardinal points by sighting on two stars rotating around the position of the celestial North Pole (b-Ursae Minoris and z-Ursae Majoris). A significant problem with Spence's theory, however, is that these stars would have been in perfect alignment in 2467 BC, whereas the most recent radiocarbon dating (as discussed in Chapter 3) suggests that Khufu's reign was about a century earlier than this date. Her hypothesis is nevertheless supported by the fact that inaccuracies in the orientations of earlier and later pyramids can be closely correlated with the degree to which the alignment of the two aforementioned stars deviates from true north.

Several well-publicized books have focused particularly on the so-called 'Orion Mystery', which is the suggestion that the layout of the three pyramids at Giza was intended to symbolize the pattern of the three stars making up the belt of Orion. The tendency of such books to focus on the undoubted astronomical elements in pyramid design allows the writers to introduce speculation concerning the possible involvement of extra-terrestrial beings in pyramid construction (which can conveniently tap into modern popular cultural ideas such as those presented in the 1995 film *Stargate*). In the late 1960s, Erich von Däniken's bestseller *Chariots of the Gods?* argued that there had been extensive extra-terrestrial influences on early human cultures. Since then, only a few writers since have gone so far as to claim that aliens may have built certain monuments, but the exploitation of astronomical aspects of the pyramids by researchers such as Robert Bauval and Graham Hancock allows them to at least imply some kind of 'outside' intervention.

Most Egyptologists argue that the real reasons for the physical form that the pyramids take must lie within the sphere of the Egyptians' own religious and funerary beliefs, as expressed in their texts and visual imagery. One possibility is that both the step-pyramid form and the true pyramid represent the primitive mound of sand, piled up over the earliest pit graves, perhaps also associated with the primeval mound of creation. Certain passages in the Pyramid Texts (inscribed on interior walls of pyramids from the late 5th Dynasty onwards) support the interpretation of the step pyramid (the earlier style, best exemplified by the 3rd-Dynasty pyramid of King Djoser at Saqqara) literally as a stairway up which the king could ascend to take his place among the stars. Elsewhere, the Pyramid Texts mention the king treading the rays of the sun in order to reach heaven, and the true pyramid might possibly therefore symbolize the rays of the sun fanning down to earth.

The above suggestions all fall within the familiar rationalist pattern, whereby Egyptologists use ancient data to explore the ways in which the ancient Egyptians themselves appear to be discussing the pyramids. Barry Kemp has summarized the way in which Egyptologists tend to use their knowledge—perhaps more 'creatively' than they are aware—when they attempt to reconstruct ancient Egyptian patterns of thought about such cultural phenomena as the pyramids:

> We can rethink ancient logic. But it creates an interesting pitfall, in that it is hard to know when to stop…We really have no way of knowing in the end if a set of scholarly guesses which might be quite true to the spirit of ancient thought and well informed of the available sources ever actually passed through the minds of the ancients at all. Modern books and scholarly articles on ancient Egyptian religion are probably adding to the original body of thought as much as explaining it in modern western terms.

Amarna issues

It is probably some kind of record (and perverse in the extreme) to have come this close to the end of a general book on ancient Egypt without having provided any detailed discussion of Nefertiti or Cleopatra—clearly among the most popular icons of ancient Egypt (the other members of this select group being of course Akhenaten and Tutankhamun). These ancient individuals, apart from being the most fascinating aspects of the subject for many modern enthusiasts, have been foremost in the transformation of Egyptology into a vibrant part of 21st-century popular culture. The ways in which these icons have been exploited can therefore give a general sense of the absorption of Egypt into the mass media.

In obedience to chronological order, we should deal with Akhenaten and Nefertiti first. Undoubtedly, Akhenaten's reign, in the mid-14th century BC, was the most unusual religious and artistic phase of the Egyptian New Kingdom (1550–1069 BC), if not the entire pharaonic period. During the first few years of his reign he appears to have developed an obsession with the cult of the Aten (literally the 'sun-disc'), a considerably more abstract deity than the traditional Egyptian pantheon. He built religious monuments to the Aten at a number of sites, but primarily at eastern Karnak and at Akhetaten ('horizon of the Aten'), the latter being a new capital city established by him on supposedly virgin ground at the site now known as Amarna in Middle Egypt. It is Amarna that has given its name to the period encompassing the reigns of Akhenaten and his brief successors. Because Akhenaten and his activities were reviled soon after his death, virtually all of his monuments were dismantled, and his name was erased from those that remained. Consequently, it was not until the work of 19th-century archaeologists that the history of the Amarna period began to be reconstructed from the many surviving fragments.

It is interesting to trace views of Akhenaten from the early 20th century onwards. Initially his stock is high, and Arthur Weigall's 'biography' of the king paints him as the founder of a 'religion so pure that one must compare it with Christianity to discover its faults', while Thomas Mann makes him the hero of his romantic novel *Joseph*, but by the 1950s Eberhard Otto was describing him as egocentric, ugly, and despotic, and in the 1980s Donald Redford argued that 'Akhenaten destroyed much, he created little...Akhenaten, whatever else he may have been, was no intellectual heavyweight'.

The high profile of Akhenaten in modern times is not so much because of any particularly detailed awareness of the architecture of his temples or his iconoclastic religious ideas (although these have had a significant impact on some more recent faiths and philosophies, such as Rosicrucianism), but because of the very striking and unusual appearance of much of the *art* of his reign. The king himself is shown as a long-faced, bulbous-chinned, thick-lipped, and fat-bellied figure, apparently with female breasts and swollen thighs, rather than being idealized as a youthful paragon of manhood as was usually the case with Egyptian kings. Akhenaten's own chief sculptor Bak claimed (in a text forming part of a rock-cut stele at Aswan) that it was the king himself who had authorized this unorthodox style of art. As in other periods, both the royal family and the elite officials surrounding the king were depicted in a similar way, thus ensuring that all those Amarna-period works of art that include human figures are fairly easy to recognize. This has led to the production of a large number of fakes and forgeries of Amarna sculptures, since the exaggerated style is also relatively easy to copy (and very popular with the buyers of antiquities). In the case of the Mansoor private collection, a large group of Amarna pieces have been subject to intense dispute concerning their authenticity. In 2003, Bolton Museum paid almost half a million pounds for a large fragment of a statuette of an Amarna princess, which had been authenticated by specialists at Christie's and the British Museum; by 2007 the sculpture had been revealed as a fake, and turned out to have been created in only three weeks in a garden shed at the home of forger Shaun Greenhalgh in Bromley Cross, Bolton.

There is also said to have been a stronger sense of freedom and creativity in Amarna art, although this perception is no doubt partly the result of the changes in religious subject matter and the survival of an unusual number of paintings from within houses and palaces as opposed to temples and tombs. It is not clear whether the artistic distortions of Amarna 'portraits' constitute a realistic record of Akhenaten's appearance (which would imply that he suffered from some form of disease) or whether there is a more symbolic reason for his androgynous appearance, perhaps relating to an attempt to personify both male and female aspects of fecundity. Some Egyptologists have suggested, for instance, that the bisexual feaures of the Amarna-style human figures might echo the form of Hapy, the god of the Nile inundation, whose body was deliberately intended to convey the idea of both male and female fertility.

The first full-blown attempt to explain Akhenaten's appearance medically was the proposal by Sir Grafton Elliot Smith that the king may have suffered from Fröhlich's Syndrome, an endocrine disorder which can have such physical effects as obesity, delayed puberty, and small testes. The disadvantage of this solution is that sufferers from this syndrome are also usually not only intellectually disabled but incapable of producing children. The latter certainly does not seem to have been the case, given that Akhenaten had at least six daughters by Nefertiti (and two further girls who seem to have resulted from incestuous relationships between the king and his own children). An alternative suggestion, first put forward by the Canadian Alwyn Burridge, is that Akhenaten might instead have suffered from Marfan's Syndrome. Quite a good case can be made for the latter (which is a severe disorder caused by a single abnormal gene), given that the symptoms include a pigeon chest, a wide pelvic area, elongated skull, spidery fingers, and a long face with protruding chin. There are still, however, many Egyptologists who quite rightly argue that such physical and medical theories take the appearance of the art far too literally, and that the peculiarities of the representations of the Amarna royal family might have lain much more within the realm of symbol and metaphor. The likelihood that we are dealing with a chosen style rather than a physical condition is backed up by surviving depictions of Akhenaten in the early part of his reign, which show him with the standard idealized features more reminiscent of his father.

All of the above factors have the effect of making Akhenaten, his wife Nefertiti, and the Amarna period endlessly fascinating to the modern observer. There are any number of 'mysteries' about the period, and constant opportunities for speculation on such topics as why Nefertiti disappears from the records before the end of Akhenaten's reign, or whether she perhaps reinvented herself as the ostensibly male ruler Smenkhkara, who enjoyed a very brief period of joint rule with Akhenaten at the end of the Amarna period. What about Akhenaten's ideology and personality? Was he a saintly monotheist who anticipated (or even precipitated) the rise of the Jewish faith, or was he an unreasonable tyrant who almost ran the Egyptian economy into the ground (or all of the above at the same time!)? One of the other burning questions concerns the fate of the corpses of the entire Amarna family. No bodies were found in the royal tomb in the desert to the east of Amarna, while the occupant of tomb KV55 in the Valley of the Kings has been much debated, with Smenkhkara and Akhenaten both being suggested as candidates for the male mummy found there. The most recent studies of the KV55 body, using such techniques as blood-group testing, molecular genetics, and macroscopic examination, strongly suggest that the body is not only that of Akhenaten, but also to be identified as the father of Tutankhamun. In 2015 Nicholas Reeves made the intriguing suggestion that Nefertiti's remains might have been placed in unexcavated annexes concealed behind two of the decorated walls of Tutankhamun's burial chamber. However, various attempts at prospection using thermo-photography and ground-penetrating radar have produced conflicting results. It remains to be seen whether these extra rooms exist, and whether, as Reeves argues, they contain a hidden burial of Nefertiti.

It was not until the late 19th century that Egyptologists became fully aware of Akhenaten and the Amarna period, but, as John Ray has pointed out, in a somewhat tongue-in-cheek assessment, the timing of Akhenaten's emergence from the shadows could not have been better:

> the 20th century turned out to be made for him: he could be seen as a tortured genius who took on a sclerotic establishment, a loving husband and father, an exceptional visionary and artist, a pacifist who believed in human brotherhood and a master of religious symbolism.

One of the tantalizing aspects of the Amarna period is that we have an enormous quantity of artistic, monumental, and textual data, and yet we still do not seem to have enough evidence to reconstruct anything like the full picture of this remarkable but relatively brief phase in Egyptian history. As Nicholas Reeves has put it, 'the real problem with Amarna is not so much a shortage of good evidence as a superabundance of speculation misrepresented as fact'.

Given Reeves's statement, it is perhaps appropriate that there have been numerous fictional rewritings of the Amarna episode, including a frightfully British rendition by Agatha Christie (*Akhnaton*) in which one of the characters observes, 'Akhnaton and I would never have got on. I don't believe he's got any sense of humour. He's so frightfully religious too.' There has even been an Amarna opera: first performed in 1984, Philip Glass's *Akhnaten* was characterized by his trademark minimalist musical style. The libretto included ancient Egyptian, Akkadian, and Hebrew, conjuring up a poignant picture of Akhenaten and Nefertiti as tragic figures, whose spirits eventually haunt the ruins of their abandoned city at Amarna. We can add to this one of the most famous Hollywood forays into ancient Egypt with *The Egyptian*, directed by Michael Curtiz in 1954; based on Mika Waltari's novel, it is set in Akhenaten's court and starred Victor Mature as Horemheb. Each of these renditions of Amarna is as idiosyncratic as the last, and the one thing they have in common is their tendency to cast Akhenaten as a revolutionary dreamer and visionary.

Icons and sirens: Egyptian femmes fatales

As if all the above were not enough, the Amarna period has yielded one particular artistic icon that somehow manages to combine the sexual attraction of Marilyn Monroe with the deadly controversy of the Elgin Marbles, along with added racism and fascism. This is of course the bust of Nefertiti (Figure 16).

The German excavator Ludwig Borchardt discovered the famous painted limestone bust of Nefertiti in 1912, in the workshop of the sculptor Thutmose, whose house was one of the large sprawling villas in the southern part of the city at Amarna. The sculpture—probably intended as a sculptor's model rather than a finished piece in itself—is about 50 cm high and fantastically well preserved, its only flaw being the absence of the right eye (although remarkably this does not particularly impair its overall beauty). The circumstances by which the bust ended up in the Berlin museum, however, have been a source of heated debate ever since. According to Nicholas Reeves,

> At the formal division of spoils a mere month after the discovery, the Nefertiti bust passed to Dr James Simon, the sponsor of the German excavations. In 1920 Simon made a formal gift of his collection to the state of Prussia; three years after that, the queen was unveiled to an astonished public—an event closely followed by

16. The bust of Queen Nefertiti (Neues Museum, Berlin), found in a sculptor's workshop at Amarna dating to *c*.1350 BC.

outraged complaints from the Egyptian Government that the
queen's portrait had left Egypt under irregular circumstances.
Accusations flew and solutions were proposed in an attempt to
resolve this unhappy situation—but to no avail...

If the bust arrived in Europe amid controversy, the situation
became worse by the 1930s, when Adolf Hitler himself declared
that it was his favourite work of art from Egypt, and would
therefore remain in Germany.

The link with Hitler is perhaps no accident, since one of the other
controversial aspects of the sculpture is the fact that it has such
characteristically European, rather than African facial
characteristics. This has meant that, for many Afrocentrists, it
symbolizes traditional Egyptologists' supposed determination to
present Egyptian culture as non-African and non-black. In the
catalogue of the polemical exhibition 'Egypt in Africa' in 1996,
Asa G. Hilliard III, Professor of Education at Georgia State
University, argued,

> This exhibit is one of the first to select items that show more typical
> African phenotypes rather than the atypical and sometimes foreign
> images that most Europeans like to see, e.g. Nefertiti, the Sheik el
> Bilad, or Kai the scribe, those ambiguous enough to be regarded
> as 'white'.

The bust seems to belong to the later part of the Amarna period,
when the new artistic style had settled down, and become much
less extreme. In the eyes of some observers it is the most
aesthetically pleasing image of a woman's face ever produced. In
an attempt to analyse why this should be the case, Jaromir Malek
suggests that

> Much of the attraction of the piece stems from its perfect, almost
> geometrical, regularity which is so appealing to our modern eyes:
> long straight lines predominate, most conspicuously those

connecting the front of the crown and the queen's forehead on profile, and the side of the crown and her cheeks on front view.

Even by the standards of 18th-Dynasty royal women, such as Ahhotep I and Hatshepsut, the real historical Nefertiti, principal wife of Akhenaten, seems to have achieved unusual power and influence, perhaps building on the achievements of her influential mother-in-law (and perhaps also aunt) Queen Tiye. The feminist Camille Paglia paints a lurid Lady-Macbeth-like portrait of Nefertiti:

> The proper response to the Nefertiti bust is fear. The queen is an android, a manufactured being. She is a new gorgoneion, a 'bodiless head of fright'…Art shows Akhenaten half-feminine, his limbs shrunken and belly bulging, possibly from birth defect or disease. This portrait shows his queen half-masculine, a vampire of political will.

Whether we agree with Paglia's characteristically over-the-top description or not, it shows the continuing power of this bust—and by extension, Nefertiti herself—to evoke passionate responses. There can be few sculptures that are so closely identified with the individual depicted that commentators discuss the bust as if it were in some sense the actual woman, which is after all a very characteristically ancient Egyptian position to take.

If Nefertiti has been exploited to some extent as a conveniently Europeanized image of Egypt, then it could be argued that something of the same sense of a bridge between Egypt and Europe can be found in the ways in which Cleopatra has been portrayed. Certainly Queen Cleopatra VII Thea Philopator, the most famous of the seven Cleopatras, long ago became such an icon and symbol of the decadent Orient that—cliché though it may be—the real woman has become increasingly difficult to find. In the immediate aftermath of the Battle of Actium and her suicide, Roman writers such as Horace and Propertius still regarded her primarily as the scheming and decadent figure who had destroyed the reputation of Mark Antony and threatened the stability of the Roman Empire, but once she was dead they could allow themselves a little more sympathy for her. In one of his odes, Horace calls her *fatale monstrum*, which can be translated literally as 'death-threatening monster', but can also have the more intriguing meaning of 'miraculous one sent by destiny', conveying the growing sense that she was a fascinating and tragic figure in her own right, rather than simply a symbol of the slothful Orient.

Even without the filmic contributions of Claudette Colbert, Vivien Leigh, and Elizabeth Taylor, Cleopatra would probably be a close rival to Nefertiti in her popular reputation for beauty, but our real knowledge of her physical appearance is actually quite tenuous (Figure 17). Indeed, when André Malraux, the French Minister of State for Cultural Affairs, was inaugurating the UNESCO Nubian Rescue Campaign in 1960, he commented that 'Cleopatra is a queen without a face'. It tends to be assumed that she was largely Greek in appearance, on the basis of her Macedonian/Ptolemaic ancestry, and the fact that she is said to have learnt Egyptian certainly implies that she was probably both racially and culturally more Greek than Egyptian. Although the 14th-century writer Giovanni Boccaccio's *De claris mulieribus* describes her as 'famous for nothing but her beauty', the portraits on contemporary coins show a woman who is distinctive rather than pretty, and Plutarch claims that 'her beauty was not in and for itself incomparable, not such to strike the person who was just looking at her; but her conversation had an irresistible charm'.

If sparkling conversation was actually the queen's best feature, it seems a shame that so few of her cinematic portrayals have had any humour in them. One of the few comedies to tackle the theme of Antony and Cleopatra was the British film *Carry on Cleo* (1964), which is perhaps best remembered for Amanda Barrie's unusually girl-next-door rendition of Cleopatra, and Kenneth

17. Bronze eighty-drachma coin of Cleopatra VII, *c*.51–30 BC, showing youthful head of Cleopatra with melon hairstyle and band-style diadem.

Williams's entirely unique version of Julius Caesar ('Infamy, infamy, they've all got it in for me!') (Figure 18).

In her cinematic incarnations Cleopatra has virtually always been played by white women, and indeed in Cecil B. DeMille's *Cleopatra* film one naive character is ridiculed for asking whether Cleopatra is black. However, as early as the 1980s there are examples of women of colour taking the role in stage productions of Shakespeare's *Antony and Cleopatra*. It is presumably because Cleopatra has become such a powerful symbol of Egypt in general that there have been attempts to claim not only that she was of

18. Poster for the British film *Carry on Cleo*, showing Amanda Barrie as Cleopatra (1964).

pure Egyptian blood but that she was a black woman. Mary Hamer, author of a book on the myth of Cleopatra, comments:

> Today controversy rages again over the body of Cleopatra and, in particular, over her race. When black nationalists in the United States lay claim to Cleopatra, as they do, that attempt is surely made in the pursuit of a dignity and respect that have been denied to black families and their way of life. Countering them are mainly white scholars, who, in defence of 'civilisation' and 'scientific knowledge', as they put it, insist that Cleopatra could not have been black.

It is primarily through the cinema and theatre (including George Bernard Shaw's *Caesar and Cleopatra*) rather than through archaeology that the reputation of Cleopatra has continued to flourish during the 20th and early 21st centuries. However, Franco-Egyptian marine archaeology in the ancient harbour areas of Alexandria has revealed many submerged sculptures and fragments of architecture from the remains of Ptolemaic and Roman buildings now on the seabed. The fact that this work is popularly described (both by archaeologists and journalists) as the excavation of 'Cleopatra's palace' is not surprising—Cleopatra is just too powerful a brand to resist (after all, both Nefertiti and Cleopatra are the names of Egyptian cigarettes). Two of the sculptures retrieved by the French marine archaeologists have been tentatively identified as Caesarion, Cleopatra's son by Julius Caesar, and another is probably Ptolemy XII, her father. It would be nice to think that somewhere on the sea floor off Alexandria there is a dazzling bust of Cleopatra to compare with the Nefertiti one in Berlin (although the face of a granite bust in the Royal Ontario Museum—widely thought to be Cleopatra—was described by the art historian Bernard Bothmer as 'dry, bland and non-committal').

Too many 'alternative Egypts'?

In this discussion of the sculpting and deconstruction of the images of Akhenaten, Nefertiti, and Cleopatra, I have concentrated primarily on the way in which they have been transformed and appropriated by artists, writers, and film-makers. Before I finish, I also need to discuss the rise of the 'alternative' Egyptologist. From the 1990s onwards, there has been a general upsurge in 'New Age' books and documentaries, some of which promoted maverick and non-academic approaches to the archaeology and texts of ancient Egypt. This is only the most recent flowering of a phenomenon that stretches further back than Egyptology itself, already encountered in the theories of such 19th-century writers as John Taylor and Charles Piazzi Smyth.

Alternative Egyptologists generally use a pick'n'mix method, selecting the data they want and ignoring or rejecting other evidence that is less conducive to their arguments. This is because they often start with an answer rather than a problem or question, then they search around for the data to prove it (not that conventional Egyptologists are entirely immune from this...). Such an approach is exactly the opposite of conventional 'problem-oriented' archaeological research techniques in which the researcher starts with a problem (e.g. what did Early Dynastic royal tombs look like?) and then explores and assesses relevant data in order to try to find one or more possible answers. One inevitable result of the pick'n'mix approach to data is that the alternative researchers occasionally use evidence that is well known or widely accepted by traditional academics. In the case of the pyramids, for instance, the information concerning the alignment of certain 'air-shafts' in the Great Pyramid with astronomical phenomena had been published by the Egyptologist I. E. S. Edwards long before Robert Bauval produced his best-selling *Orion Mystery* (which suggested that the layout of the three Giza pyramids was intended to replicate the arrangement of stars in the Orion constellation, while one of the southern air-shafts was aligned with the brightest star in Orion). Similarly, the visual links between the sites of Heliopolis and Giza, taking the form of demonstrable sight-lines between the monuments, were studied and described by University College London lecturer David Jeffreys, as well as forming part of Bauval's hypothesis.

Within the scope of this book, devoted mainly to the archaeology and history of ancient Egypt, I have only been able to dip my toe occasionally into the vast ocean of alternative approaches to Egypt, and the ways in which Egyptian ideas, motifs, and stories have been reworked and reappropriated by modern artists, architects, writers, musicians, and dramatists. The alternative Egypts, from Boris Karloff's resurrected mummy to Bernal's 'Black Athena' and Philip Glass's operatic *Akhnaten*, deserve several books all to themselves. The 'wonderful things' quote attributed to Howard Carter when asked by Lord Carnarvon what he could see when he looked into the burial chamber of Tutankhamun is part of the high camp charm not only of ancient Egypt but also of Egyptology itself. Europeans and Americans wearing pith helmets, riding on camels, posing in their Edwardian best suits outside royal tombs, and dressing up in Ottoman finery have become as much part of our modern mental view of Egypt as all the surviving ancient images. In addition, of course, our contemporary images now also draw on *Stargate*, Tomb Raider, Indiana Jones, and any number of video games and animations exploiting ancient Egyptian source material.

Chapter 10
Cultural heritage

Journalists often like to compare modern presidents of Egypt with the ancient pharaohs, and it's always difficult to know whether there really are any parallels buried in these media clichés. Certainly it is difficult to imagine that the events of the so-called Arab Spring had any genuine counterparts in the pharaonic period. What we know for certain is that the popular uprising in 2011 led to the end of the very long period of Hosni Mubarak's rule over Egypt (which had entirely dominated my own archaeological career in Egypt since the 1980s) as well as triggering the beginning of something else in political and social terms. This is not the place to discuss the pros and cons of the brief presidency of Mohammed Morsi, or indeed the current regime led by Abdel Fattah el-Sisi (tempting though this is), but in this chapter I would like to discuss the various impacts of these processes of socio-economic and political change on pharaonic cultural heritage, especially its archaeological sites and museums.

Political unrest and cultural heritage

One immediate effect of the political events in Egypt in 2011 was a decline in law and order that triggered off a significant amount of looting of archaeological sites and finds-stores. The first real indication of any threat to Egyptian heritage arrived on 28 January 2011, when protesters set fire to the headquarters of the ruling National Democratic Party in downtown Cairo. Since this building was immediately next door to the Egyptian Museum, there were soon reports on television and social media that the museum itself was on fire—these rumours fortunately turned out not to be true, but the museum nevertheless became one of the most publicized looting targets (despite Egyptian protesters famously forming a human chain around it). The manner of the raid was along the lines of a Hollywood heist—a group of ten men entered the museum on ropes through glass panes on the roof breaking about seventy objects in the process, and stealing some sixty pieces (reports vary wildly on these statistics for breakages and theft), including several items from the tomb of Tutankhamun. Astonishingly at least twenty-five of the stolen objects were subsequently recovered by Egypt's Tourism and Antiquities police, including a limestone statuette of Akhenaten reportedly found beside a rubbish bin, and four items discovered in a bag mysteriously left in a Cairo metro station less than two months later. These bizarre events have led to some speculation that both thefts and recoveries were perhaps some kind of inside job, but the real facts will probably never be known.

Due to continued political instability, two years after the Egyptian Museum thefts, the civil unrest was still so severe that the Mallawi Museum, in Middle Egypt, for instance, was stormed and totally looted by armed robbers. Over the same two-year period, many of Egypt's archaeological sites, as well as their local store-rooms (each containing thousands of finds), were subject to repeated thefts (Figure 19). Egypt's pharaonic cultural heritage was therefore arguably under its greatest threat since the days when 19th-century Western visitors were allowed to strip many sites of their treasures. It's very important to remember, however, that, although Egyptians may often have been physically responsible for the thefts, the root of the problem has always lain not with local so-called 'subsistence diggers' but with antiquities-traders, private collectors, and sometimes even museums, based in a whole myriad of places outside Egypt.

19. The author (climbing ladder) assessing damage to a New Kingdom tomb looted at the site of Gurob in 2011.

As Neil Brodie had already pointed out (in a book written about six years before the Arab Spring):

> Some of the worst examples of archaeological looting...have occurred in countries suffering from the public disorder and economic disruption that follow the breakdown of central authority...In these circumstances, law enforcement is weak and buried artifacts are a ready source of cash for people who have seen their homes and their livelihoods destroyed.

Brodie was referring primarily to conditions brought on by war, such as the 1991 and 2003 conflicts in Iraq, but his comments are equally applicable to Egypt in the early 2010s, which experienced long periods when police and security forces were absent from large areas of the country. It is always easier to blame the looters rather than the international system that they are feeding. The experience at some archaeological sites, however, strongly suggests that 'cherry-picking' collectors exploited the situation in Egypt in 2011–13 to target and remove specific items. At Wadi Hammamat, for instance, only a short walk from the quarries that produced the Narmer Palette, a rock-cut inscription was removed from a very difficult, high location on the rock-face (as opposed to others that would have been much easier and quicker to remove), probably because it consisted of an unusual Persian-period genealogical text (Figure 20).

The pursuit and sale of antiquities is comparable with illegal international trade in drugs or arms, although a major difference is that the ultimate purchasers of stolen antiquities very often do so openly and apparently legally, relying on so-called 'market nations' (such as Hong Kong, Singapore, and Thailand) that have often not ratified such international agreements as the 1970 UNESCO Convention on Cultural Property. These market nations serve as transit points, effectively laundering the artefacts and imparting legitimacy to their onward trafficking, usually at prices

20. Rock-face at Wadi Hammamat, showing (left) a Persian-period genealogical text still intact, and (right) the same piece of rock-face after the theft of the text in 2011.

that are at least a hundred times higher than the money earned by the local looter.

As with other countries that have been particularly affected by the illicit trade in antiquities (such as Iraq, Peru, and Guatemala), the real culprits are the dealers and collectors in the so-called 'destination markets', and the true solutions lie not only in tighter enforcement of antiquities laws but also in much broader aspects of international economics and capitalism—as Brodie puts it:

> Subsistence digging will stop only when rural populations are in
> safe possession of their own land and are able to receive a fair price
> for their agricultural produce, which in turn requires the abolition
> of tariffs and other trade barriers.

Threats to Egypt's pharaonic cultural heritage during the period from 2011 to 2014 were not restricted to theft from museums or sites—there was also the phenomenon of 'land-grabbing' (the illegal taking of land owned by the Ministry for Antiquities) either for agriculture or building projects—this took place at a number of well-known archaeological areas, such as the Predynastic cemetery of Tarkhan and the New Kingdom city of Amarna. It is important, however, to consider the real social backdrop to these problems, especially given that many contemporary Egyptian communities may desperately need to expand either for economic reasons or in order to create new cemeteries. Foreign missions working on pharaonic period sites sometimes also bear considerable responsibility for the situation not only because they often fail to engage and involve local communities with their work, but also because their research is rarely disseminated locally. The unfortunate lack of resources in the Ministry of Antiquities for fully maintaining and updating records of archaeological sites only serves to add to the confusion and feelings of local disconnection. If we are to achieve a balance between conservation and the need for modern populations to flourish, more impetus needs to be put into community-based initiatives of engagement with their cultural heritage. Problems with cultural heritage and antiquities trafficking are inextricably tied up with numerous other social and political factors.

Innovative approaches to cultural heritage management in Egypt

It might be argued, paradoxically, that one effect of the temporary increase in looting and land-grabbing in the period from 2011 to 2013 was to create a new can-do spirit among many archaeologists and other stakeholders in Egypt. This led to some benefits by highlighting the need for long-term cultural heritage planning in a whole variety of sites and regions. There is, however, a continued severe lack of sustainable, long-term strategies for cultural heritage management in Egypt.

At Esna, for example, the main tourist attraction is the Graeco-Roman Temple of Khnum (which is a World Heritage site), but a report published in 2015 by Marwa Ghanem and Samar Saad indicated that the well-intentioned plan for Sustainable Heritage Tourism (SHT) there had failed miserably. By conducting interviews with the various stakeholders, such as local residents, travel company managers, government officials responsible for tourism, and academics involved in excavations at the temple, they were able to establish some of the reasons for the failure of the SHT plan. These problems included lack of communication between local residents and officials in charge of tourism, lack of control over new building projects in the archaeological areas of the city, and the creation of a new Nile barrage in 2008, which speeded up river traffic and therefore meant that cruise boats no longer stopped for long periods to use the local markets and other amenities in Esna. In addition, the report found that conflict between different branches of local government had resulted in a failure to solve groundwater and sewage problems that were causing the temple to deteriorate. Ghanem and Saad point out the crucial importance, in any future plan for Esna, of adopting holistic, inclusive strategies that are particularly geared towards convincing the residents of the economic and social value of maintaining and enhancing their own local heritage:

> The desperate populace, due to poverty and ignorance, began to infringe their cultural heritage through theft to earn their living. In order for promotional activities to be fruitful, the people should be convinced that their long-term financial wellbeing depends on the adoption of sustainable development in the Temple site.

Similar problems beset attempts to create a proper cultural heritage strategy for the site of the Giza pyramids—the scheme there has so far largely failed not because of any lack of money but due partly to failure to properly consult and involve the local people.

There are, however, some indications of possible fruitful and innovative ways forward, some of which are discussed by Elizabeth Bloxam and Adel Kelany in a recent assessment of best practice in Egyptian cultural heritage management. They point out the degree to which approaches to such management have tended to follow heavily Western models that are often inappropriate. Instead, they stress the need for:

> 'bottom up' thinking, rather than communities responding to expert-driven agendas in which defining heritage values, often at a global scale, simply detaches local people from the process.

Bloxam and Kelany point out that many of the more fruitful areas in recent years have lain within the sphere of post-pharaonic Islamic cultural heritage and a few non-monumental archaeological landscapes. An example of good practice in Islamic heritage management is the Al-Azhar Park Project (created by the Aga Khan Development Network), which led to the creation of a thirty-million-dollar park incorporating a range of historic Islamic buildings. In stark contrast to the situation in Esna and Giza, local people (in the neighbouring Darb al-Ahmar community) were incorporated into the whole ongoing Al-Azhar project through financing of new local businesses and support for restoration of numerous Islamic buildings that had fallen into disrepair, thus giving residents a real economic and social stake in their own heritage.

Another example of a successful 'bottom up', community-based heritage plan was developed at Aswan in 2006, when the Egyptian Ministry of Antiquities created an Ancient Quarries and Mines Department (AQMD) led by Adel Kelany. This initiative, supervised entirely by local Egyptian archaeologists in Aswan, has been building up a database of sites in the Aswan region relating to ancient quarrying and mining, but crucially the AQMD team has also liaised with local people and contractors to raise awareness of a wide range of types of site, such as rock art and ancient settlement remains, thus helping to ensure their survival. The strategies developed locally by AQMD have enabled them both to control the issuing of official permits for modern quarrying and mining activities, and—in cases where the modern interference appears to be unstoppable—to ensure that archaeological surveys are undertaken in advance of any work.

Egypt's new museums

Until very recently the vast majority of ancient Egyptian objects on display in Egypt itself were concentrated in a very small number of large museums in Cairo, Alexandria, Luxor, and Aswan. Gradually, however, in the early 21st century, a number of smaller regional museums have either been newly established or greatly enhanced (such as the open-air Merenptah Museum inaugurated at Luxor in 2001, the Imhotep Museum opened at Saqqara in 2006, and the pyramid-shaped 'Akhenaten Museum' at Minya, scheduled for completion in 2021). These small local museums have often been created so as to display objects closer to the sites from which they were excavated; this has also resulted in many items from the big central collections being redistributed to regional museums in order to fill key chronological gaps. The strategy of increasing the quantity of material on display locally is designed to try to persuade organized tours to spend time and money in smaller Egyptian towns and cities that have not tended to benefit so much from cultural tourism. Time will tell whether this policy bears fruit in future, given the continued tendency of foreign tourists to cluster in Cairo, Luxor, and Aswan, or on the Red Sea coast.

Some Egyptian scholars, however, have questioned whether the new provincial museums are being created within any kind of coherent overall framework, and indeed two Egyptian museum specialists, Maher Eissa and Louay Saied, have questioned the very basis of the strategy:

> During the past few decades, the Antiquities authorities have established several museums, without a clear and precise philosophy or policy on the role and aim of these museums. As a result, conflicts of interest have arisen between new museums, simply because there is no common 'collection policy' to be followed. Fundamentally, there was no vision of the real requirements of building new museums, specifically the regional ones.

During the same time that these regional museum projects have been progressing, nearly 800 million US dollars have been spent during the 2010s on the creation of a huge new project near the Giza pyramids, known as the Grand Egyptian Museum (GEM). This new national museum is planned to display over 100,000 objects in a 480,000-square-metre complex, including the Tutankhamun collection (which has so far been displayed at the Egyptian Museum in central Cairo). The Narmer Palette itself is no doubt also on the move—due to be transferred to the GEM sometime soon, along with other iconic masterpieces. The expectation is that the GEM will be visited by somewhere between five and eight million tourists (based on the projection that it will lead to an increase of 30 per cent in tourist numbers overall). Like any mega-project, it is of course not without controversy, and there are many scholars who might have preferred a major make-over on the existing neo-classical Egyptian Museum in Tahrir Square (which was created in 1902), thus perhaps allowing more money to be spent on smaller provincial projects like those described above. The GEM has also taken a lot longer to complete than originally planned—the original design was approved in 2002, and building began in 2005, however the final opening date has receded ever further into the distance (2022 being optimistically suggested as its opening date at the time of writing).

So where does this leave us? There are some small beacons of hope in terms of museums and cultural heritage management in Egypt, but the landscape as a whole is in a state of flux and generally lacking an overall strategic framework, particularly one that is sustainable and designed to accommodate the diverse needs of local communities in Egypt. In the end, Egypt's pharaonic past is inextricably connected to its present, and these two cultural spheres must gradually find better, more innovative ways in which to interact and coexist.

Timeline

Prehistory	
Palaeolithic	*c.*700,000–10,000 BP
Epipalaeolithic	*c.*10,000–7000 BP
Neolithic	*c.*5300–4000 BC
Badarian period	*c.*4400–4000
Naqada I period	*c.*4000–3600
Naqada II period	*c.*3600–3350
Naqada III/'Dynasty 0'	*c.*3350–3000
Pharaonic/Dynastic Period	3000–332 BC
Early Dynastic Period	**3000–2686**
1st Dynasty	3000–2890
2nd Dynasty	2890–2686
Old Kingdom	**2686–2181**
3rd Dynasty	2686–2613
4th Dynasty	2613–2494
5th Dynasty	2494–2345
6th Dynasty	2345–2181
First Intermediate Period	**2181–2055**
7th and 8th Dynasties	2181–2125

9th and 10th Dynasties	2160–2025
11th Dynasty (Thebes only)	2125–2055
Middle Kingdom	**2055–1650**
11th Dynasty (all Egypt)	2055–1985
12th Dynasty	1985–1795
13th Dynasty	1795–after 1650
14th Dynasty	1750–1650
Second Intermediate Period	**1650–1550**
15th Dynasty (Hyksos)	1650–1550
16th Dynasty (minor Hyksos)	1650–1550
17th Dynasty (Theban)	1650–1550
New Kingdom	**1550–1069**
18th Dynasty	1550–1295
Ramessid period	1295–1069
19th Dynasty	1295–1186
20th Dynasty	1186–1069
Third Intermediate Period	**1069–664**
21st Dynasty	1069–945
22nd Dynasty	945–715
23rd Dynasty	818–715
24th Dynasty	727–715
25th Dynasty (Kushite)	747–656
Late Period	**664–332**
26th Dynasty (Saite)	664–526
27th Dynasty (1st Persian period)	526–404
28th Dynasty	404–399
29th Dynasty	399–380
30th Dynasty	380–340

2nd Persian period	340–332
Ptolemaic Period	**332–30 bc**
Macedonian Dynasty	332–305
Cleopatra VII Philopator	51–30
Roman Period	30 BC–AD 311

Glossary

akh: the form in which the blessed dead inhabited the underworld, and also the result of the successful reunion of an individual's *ba* with his/her *ka*.

Aten: deity represented in the form of the disc or orb of the sun, the cult of which was particularly promoted during the reign of Akhenaten.

***ba*, *ba*-bird:** aspect of human beings that resembles our concept of 'personality', comprising the non-physical attributes which made each person unique; often depicted as a bird with a human head and arms, and also used to refer to the physical manifestations of certain gods.

Books of the Netherworld/Book of the Dead: The netherworld texts comprise a number of related funerary writings, which together were known to the Egyptians as Amduat or 'that which is in the Netherworld'. They included the *Book of Caverns*, *Book of Gates*, and the *Writing of the Hidden Chamber*. The theme of all of these works is the journey of the sun god through the realms of darkness during the twelve hours of the night, leading up to his triumphant rebirth with the dawn each morning. The above examples were found in royal tombs primarily during the New Kingdom, but a more widespread example, known from the Second Intermediate Period onwards, was the *Book of Dead*, frequently inscribed on papyrus and placed with both royal and non-royal burials.

BP: abbreviation for 'before present', which is most commonly used for uncalibrated radiocarbon dates or thermoluminescence dates. 'Present' is conventionally taken to be AD 1950.

cartouche *(shenu)*: elliptical outline representing a length of knotted rope with which certain elements of the Egyptian royal titulary were surrounded from the 4th Dynasty onwards.

Coffin Texts: group of over a thousand spells, selections from which were inscribed on coffins during the Middle Kingdom.

demotic: cursive script (Greek, 'popular (script)') known to the Egyptians as *sekh shat*, which replaced the *hieratic* script by the 26th Dynasty. Initially used only in commercial and bureaucratic documents, by the Ptolemaic period it was also being used for religious, scientific, and literary texts.

false door: stone or wooden architectural element comprising a rectangular imitation door placed inside Egyptian non-royal tomb-chapels. Funerary offerings were usually placed in front of false doors.

hieratic: cursive script used from at least the end of the Early Dynastic period onwards, enabling scribes to write more rapidly on papyri and ostraca, making it the preferred medium for scribal tuition (Greek *hieratika*, 'sacred'). An even more cursive form of the script, known as 'abnormal hieratic', began to be used for business texts in Upper Egypt during the Third Intermediate Period.

hieroglyphics: script consisting of pictograms, ideograms, and phonograms arranged in horizontal and vertical lines (Greek, 'sacred carved (letters)'), which was in use from the late Predynastic period (*c*.3200 BC) to the late 4th century AD.

Horus name: the first royal name in the sequence of five names making up the Egyptian royal titulary, usually written inside a *serekh*.

instruction: type of literary text (e.g. *The Instruction of Amenemhat I*) consisting of aphorisms and ethical advice (Egyptian *sebayt*, 'wisdom texts', 'didactic literature').

ka: the creative life-force of any individual, whether human or divine. Represented by a hieroglyph consisting of a pair of arms, it was considered to be the essential ingredient that differentiated a living person from a dead one.

maat: Egyptian concept relating to justice, truth, and universal harmony. The idea was personified by the goddess Maat, usually depicted either as an ostrich feather or as a seated woman wearing such a feather on her head.

***mastaba*-tomb:** type of Egyptian tomb, the rectangular superstructure of which resembles the low mud-brick benches outside Egyptian houses (Arabic, 'bench'). It was used for both royal and non-royal burials in the Early Dynastic Period but only for non-royal burials from the Old Kingdom onwards.

Maya: Mesoamerican people and culture who flourished *c.* AD 200–850.

nome: Greek term used to refer to the forty-two traditional provinces of Egypt, which the ancient Egyptians themselves called *sepat*. For most of the dynastic period, there were twenty-two Upper Egyptian and twenty Lower Egyptian nomes.

nomen: birth name; royal name introduced by the epithet *sa-Ra* ('son of Ra'). Usually the last one in the sequence of the royal titulary, it was the only one given to the pharaoh as soon as he was born.

ostracon (plural: ostraca): sherd of pottery or flake of limestone bearing texts and drawings, commonly consisting of personal jottings, letters, sketches, or scribal exercises, but sometimes also inscribed with literary texts, usually in the *hieratic* script (Greek *ostrakon*, pl. *ostraka*; 'potsherd').

playa: plain or depression where run-off from surrounding highlands collects, forming an ephemeral lake. When dry, the playa, sometimes containing archaeological deposits, is subject to aeolian processes of erosion and deposition.

prenomen: throne name; one of the five names in the Egyptian royal titulary, which was introduced by the title *nesu-bit* 'he of the sedge and the bee', which is a reference both to the individual mortal king and the eternal kingship (not 'king of Upper and Lower Egypt', as it is sometimes erroneously translated).

pylon: massive ceremonial gateway (Greek, 'gate'), called *bekhenet* by the Egyptians, which consisted of two tapering towers linked by a bridge of masonry and surmounted by a cornice. It was used in temples from at least the Middle Kingdom to the Roman period.

Pyramid Texts: the earliest Egyptian funerary texts, comprising some 800 spells or 'utterances' written in columns on the walls of the corridors and burial chambers of nine pyramids of the late Old Kingdom and First Intermediate Period.

satrapy: province in the Achaemenid (Persian) Empire.

serekh: rectangular panel (perhaps representing a palace gateway) surmounted by the Horus falcon (or the Seth jackal), within which the king's 'Horus name' was written.

seriation: method of arranging artefacts, sites, or assemblages into a linear sequence on the basis of the degree of similarity between the various elements in the sequence (e.g. developments in artefactual style, function, or material).

sistrum: musical rattling instrument (Egyptian *seshesht*; Greek *seistron*) played mainly by women, but also by the pharaoh when making offerings to the goddess Hathor.

vizier: term used to refer to the holders of the Egyptian title *tjaty*, whose position is considered to have been roughly comparable with that of the vizier (or chief minister) in the Ottoman Empire. The vizier was therefore usually the next most powerful person after the king.

References

Chapter 1: Introduction

Jan Assmann, *Moses the Egyptian* (Cambridge, Mass., 1997), p. 209

Barry Kemp, *Ancient Egypt: Anatomy of a Civilization*, 3rd edn (London, 2018), p. 3

John Romer, *Testament: The Bible and History* (London, 1988), p. 71

Bruce Trigger, 'The Narmer Palette in Cross-Cultural Perspective', in Manfred Görg and Edgar Pusch (eds), *Festschrift Elmar Edel* (Bamberg, 1979), p. 415

Bruce Trigger, *A History of Archaeological Thought* (Cambridge, 1989), pp. 200–2

John Wortham, *British Egyptology: 1549–1906* (Newton Abbot, 1971), p. 106

Chapter 2: Reconstructing ancient Egypt

Elizabeth Bloxam, '"A Place Full of Whispers": Socializing the Quarry Landscape of the Wadi Hammamat' *Cambridge Archaeological Journal* 25/4 (2015), p. 797

Michael Hoffman, *Egypt before the Pharaohs* (London, 1979), p. 129

John Laughlin, *Archaeology and the Bible* (London, 2000), p. 85

James Quibell and Frederick Green, *Hierakonpolis II* (London, 1902), p. 30

Archibald Sayce, *The Archaeology of the Cuneiform Inscriptions*, 2nd edn (London, 1908), p. 188

Chapter 3: History

Donald Redford, *Pharaonic King-lists, Annals and Day-Books: A Contribution to the Egyptian Sense of History* (Mississauga, 1986), p. xix

Chapter 4: Writing

Walter Fairservis Jr, 'A Revised View of the Na'rmr Palette', *Journal of the American Research Center in Egypt* 28 (1991), pp. 1–20

Alan Gardiner, *Egypt of the Pharaohs* (Oxford, 1961), p. 404

Barry Kemp, 'Large Middle Kingdom Granary Buildings (and the Archaeology of Administration)', *Zeitschrift für Ägyptische Sprache und Altertumskunde* 113 (1986), pp. 120–36

Andréas Stauder, 'Scripts', in Ian Shaw and Elizabeth Bloxam (eds), *The Oxford Handbook of Egyptology* (Oxford, 2020), p. 873

Chapter 5: Kingship

Alan Gardiner, *Egypt of the Pharaohs* (Oxford, 1961), p. 198

Nicolas Grimal, *A History of Ancient Egypt*, tr. Ian Shaw (Oxford, 1992), p. 212

Suzanne Ratié, *La Reine Hatchepsout: Sources et problèmes* (Leiden, 1979), p. 264

Donald Redford, *History and Chronology of the Eighteenth Dynasty of Egypt* (Toronto, 1967), pp. 63–4, 85–6

John Wilson, *The Burden of Egypt* (Chicago, 1951), pp. 174–5

Chapter 6: Identity

Charles Loring Brace et al., 'Clines and Clusters versus Race: A Test in Ancient Egypt and the Case of a Death on the Nile', in Mary R. Lefkowitz and Guy M. Roberts (eds), *Black Athena Revisited* (Chapel Hill, NC, and London, 1996), p. 162

Nadine Cherpion, 'Deux manucures royaux de la Ve dynastie', in A. Theodorides et al. (eds), *Archéologie et philologie dans les études des civilisations orientales* (Leuven, 1986), p. 67

Tom Hare, *ReMembering Osiris* (Stanford, Calif., 1999), pp. 139, 144

Sarah Morris, 'The Legacy of Black Athena', in Mary R. Lefkowitz and Guy M. Roberts (eds), *Black Athena Revisited* (Chapel Hill, NC, and London, 1996), p. 162

Lynn Meskell, 'Desperately Seeking Gender: A Review Article', *Archaeological Review from Cambridge* 13/1 (1994), p. 109

Grafton Elliot Smith, 'Anatomical Report', *Archaeological Survey of Nubia Bulletin* 3 (1909), p. 25

Chapter 7: Death

Mark Smith, 'Democratization of the Afterlife', in Jacco Dieleman and Willeke Wendrich (eds), *UCLA Encyclopedia of Egyptology* (Los Angeles, 2009). [<http://digital2.library.ucla.edu/viewItem.do?ark=21198/zz001nf62b>. Accessed 15 June 2020]

John Wilson, *The Culture of Ancient Egypt* (Chicago, 1951), p. 87

Chapter 8: Religion

Nicolas Grimal, *A History of Ancient Egypt*, tr. I. Shaw (Oxford, 1992), p. 142 (Ankhtifi's biography)

Tom Hare, *ReMembering Osiris* (Stanford, Calif., 1999), p. 145

Erik Hornung, *Conceptions of God in Ancient Egypt: The One and The Many*, tr. J. Baines (London, 1982), pp. 255–6

Erik Hornung, *Idea into Image: Essays on Ancient Egyptian Thought* (Princeton, 1992), p. 13

Barry Kemp, 'How Religious were the Ancient Egyptians?', *Cambridge Archaeological Journal* 5/1 (1995), p. 26

Chapter 9: Egyptomania

Mary Hamer, 'The Myth of Cleopatra since the Renaissance', in S. Walker and P. Higgs (eds), *Cleopatra of Egypt: From History to Myth* (London, 2001), p. 310

Asa G. Hilliard III, 'Are Africans African? Scholarship over Rhetoric and Propaganda. Valid Discourse on Kemetic Origins', in Theodore Celenko (ed.), *Egypt in Africa* (Indianapolis, 1996), p. 113

Barry Kemp, *Ancient Egypt: Anatomy of a Civilization*, 1st edn (London, 1989), pp. 4–5

Jaromir Malek, *Egypt: 4000 Years of Art* (London, 2003), p. 190

André Malraux, 'The Action of a Man who Snatches Something from Death', *The UNESCO Courier*, May 1960 [<https://en.unesco.org/courier/may-1960/andre-malraux-action-man-who-snatches-something-death>. Accessed 15 June 2020]

Auguste Mariette, *Notice des principaux monuments exposés dans les galeries provisoires du Musée d'Antiquités Égyptiennes de S. A. Le vice-roi, à Boulaq* (Alexandria, 1864), p. 8

Camille Paglia, *Sexual Personae: Art and Decadence from Nefertiti to Emily Dickinson* (New York, 1991), pp. 68–9

John Ray, 'Akhenaten: Hero or Heretic', *The Times* (London, 21 Mar. 2001)

Donald Redford, 'Monotheism of a Heretic', *Biblical Archaeology Review* 13/3 (1987), p. 28

Nicholas Reeves, *Ancient Egypt: The Great Discoveries* (London, 2000), p. 136

Nicholas Reeves, *Akhenaten: Egypt's False Prophet* (London, 2001), p. 9

Arthur Weigall, *The Life and Times of Akhnaten, Pharaoh of Egypt*, 4th edn (Edinburgh, 1922), p. 53

Chapter 10: Cultural heritage

Neil Brodie, Morag M. Kersel, Christina Luke, and Kathryn Walker Tubb, *Archaeology, Cultural Heritage, and the Antiquities Trade* (Gainesville, Fla., 1989), pp. 5–6

Maher Eissa and Louay Saied, 'Museum Collections and Moving Objects in Egypt: An Approach to Amend the Current Situation', in Patrizia Piacentini et al. (eds), *Forming Material Egypt* (Milan, 2013), p. 82

Marwa Ghanem and Samar Saad, 'Enhancing Sustainable Heritage Tourism in Egypt: Challenges and Framework of Action', *Journal of Heritage Tourism* 10/4 (2015), p. 373

Further reading

Preface

Numerous books and articles discuss the Narmer Palette and other protodynastic palettes and mace-heads. A few of the more interesting ones are: James Quibell and Frederick Green, *Hierakonpolis*, 2 vols (London, 1900–2); Elise J. Baumgartel, *The Cultures of Prehistoric Egypt II* (London, 1960); Bruce Trigger, 'The Narmer Palette in Cross-Cultural Perspective', in Manfred Görg and Edgar Pusch (eds), *Festschrift Elmar Edel* (Bamberg, 1979), pp. 409–19; Whitney Davis, *Masking the Blow* (Berkeley, 1992); David Wengrow, 'Rethinking "Cattle Cults" in Early Egypt: Towards a Prehistoric Perspective on the Narmer Palette', *Cambridge Archaeological Journal* 11/1 (2001), pp. 91–104; David O'Connor, 'The Narmer Palette: A New Interpretation', in Emily Teeter (ed.), *Before The Pyramids: The Origins of Egyptian Civilization* (Chicago, 2011), pp. 145–52; and Jorrit Kelder, 'Narmer, Scorpion and the Representation of the Early Egyptian Royal Court', *Origini: Preistoria e protostoria delle civiltà antiche* 35 (2013), pp. 143–56.

Chapter 1: Introduction

The following general works present a good range of different perspectives on ancient Egypt: David Wengrow, *The Archaeology of Early Egypt* (Cambridge, 2006); Willeke Wendrich (ed.), *Egyptian Archaeology* (London, 2010); Barry Kemp, *Ancient Egypt: Anatomy of a Civilization*, 3rd edn (London, 2018); Ian Shaw and

Elizabeth Bloxam (eds), *The Oxford Handbook of Egyptology* (Oxford, 2020).

For the Taramsa Hill Palaeolithic human remains, see Pierre Vermeersch et al., 'A Middle Palaeolithic Burial of a Modern Human at Taramsa Hill, Egypt', *Antiquity* 72 (1988), pp. 475–84.

For Egypt and the Greeks see Alan Lloyd, *Herodotus Book II.1: An Introduction* (Leiden, 1975); Alan K. Bowman, *Egypt after the Pharaohs* (London, 1986); Naphthali Lewis, *Greeks in Ptolemaic Egypt* (Oxford, 1986); Roger Matthews and Cornelia Roemer, *Ancient Perspectives on Egypt* (London, 2003); A. Villing and U. Schlotzhauer (eds), *Naukratis: Greek Diversity in Egypt: Studies on East Greek Pottery and Exchange in the Eastern Mediterranean* (London, 2006).

For Egypt and the Bible, see Donald Redford, *A Study of the Biblical Story of Joseph (Genesis 37–50)* (Leiden, 1970); Anson F. Rainey (ed.), *Egypt, Israel, Sinai: Archaeological and Historical Relationships in the Biblical Period* (Tel Aviv, 1987); John Romer, *Testament: The Bible and History* (London, 1988); and Donald Redford, *Egypt, Canaan and Israel in Ancient Times* (Princeton, 1992). An English translation of Sigmund Freud's *Moses and Monotheism* is to be found in volume XXIII in James Strachey's standard edition of the *Complete Psychological Works of Sigmund Freud* (London, 1955). For the arguments against Ramesses II being the Exodus pharaoh, see Farouk Gomaa, *Chaemwese, Sohn Ramses' II. und Hohenpriester von Memphis* (Wiesbaden, 1973). For the 18th-Dynasty pedestal in Berlin perhaps mentioning Israel, see Manfred Görg, Peter van der Veen, and Christoffer Theis, 'When Did Ancient Israel Begin?', *Biblical Archaeology Review* 38/1 (2012), pp. 59–62.

For the history of Egyptology, see Andrew Bednarski, Salima Ikram, and Aidan Dodson, *A History of World Egyptology* (Cambridge, 2020), and for the *Description de l'Egypte* specifically, see Andrew Bednarski, *Holding Egypt: Tracing the Reception of the* Description de l'Égypte *in Nineteenth-Century Great Britain* (London, 2005).

For Flinders Petrie's system of 'sequence dating' for the Predynastic, see his own exposition of the technique in *Diospolis Parva* (London, 1901), and see also Stan Hendrickx, 'Predynastic-Early Dynastic Chronology', in Erik Hornung, Rolf Krauss, and David Warburton (eds), *Ancient Egyptian Chronology* (Leiden, 2006), pp. 53–93.

Chapter 2: Reconstructing ancient Egypt

For discussion of the early discovery of ancient Egypt see David O'Connor, 'Egyptology and Archaeology: An African Perspective', in Peter Robertshaw (ed.), *A History of African Archaeology* (Portsmouth and London, 1990), pp. 236–51; Jean Vercoutter, *The Search for Ancient Egypt* (London, 1992); Nicholas Reeves, *Ancient Egypt: The Great Discoveries* (London, 2000). For discussion of the functions and decorative programmes of each face of the protodynastic ceremonial palettes, see David O'Connor, 'Context, Function and Program: Understanding Ceremonial Slate Palettes', *Journal of the American Research Center in Egypt* 39 (2002), pp. 5–25.

For the 'Minoan' paintings at Tell el-Dab'a see Vivian Davies and Louise Schofield (eds), *Egypt, the Aegean and the Levant* (London, 1995), and Manfred Bietak, 'Egypt and the Aegean: Cultural Convergence in a Thutmoside Palace at Avaris', in Catharine H. Roehrig (ed.), *Hatshepsut: From Queen to Pharaoh* (New York and New Haven, 2005), pp. 75–81; and, for a broader perspective on Minoan-style art across the East Mediterranean, see Ann Brysbaert, *The Power of Technology in the Bronze Age Eastern Mediterranean: The Case of the Painted Plaster* (London, 2009).

For multidisciplinary studies of the Amarna Letters see Raymond Cohen and Raymond Westbrook (eds), *Amarna Diplomacy* (Baltimore and London, 2000) and for the latest translation and discussions, see Anson F. Rainey (ed.) *The El-Amarna Correspondence: A New Edition of the Cuneiform Letters from the Site of el-Amarna Based on Collations of All Extant Tablets* (Leiden, 2015). Detailed discussion of the scientific analysis of the Amarna tablets' clays can be found in Yuval Goren, Israel Finkelstein, and Nadav Na'aman, *Inscribed in Clay: Provenance Study of the Amarna Letters and Other Ancient Near Eastern Texts* (Tel Aviv, 2004).

Alfred Lucas's pioneering examination of materials and craftwork in ancient Egypt was first published in 1926, reprinted several times, and eventually lightly revised by John Harris: *Ancient Egyptian Materials and Industries*, 4th edn (London, 1962). It was the only book on the topic for nearly eighty years, until the publication of Paul Nicholson and Ian Shaw (eds), *Ancient Egyptian Materials and Technology* (Cambridge, 2000). For an interesting summary of early scientific techniques in Egyptology, see Eric Peet, *The Present State of Egyptological Studies* (Oxford, 1934) and for more recent assessments of the state of play, see Ian Shaw, *Ancient Egyptian Technology and Innovation: Transformations in Pharaonic Material Culture* (London, 2012), and Sonia Zakrzewski, Andrew Shortland, and Joanne Rowland, *Science in the Study of Ancient Egypt* (London and New York, 2015).

For work at the Wadi Hammamat quarries, see Elizabeth Bloxam, James Harrell, Adel Kelany, Norah Moloney, Ashraf el-Senussi, and Adel Tohamey, 'Investigating the Predynastic Origins of Greywacke Working in the Wadi Hammamat', *Archéonil* 24 (2014), pp. 11–30; Elizabeth Bloxam, '"A Place Full of Whispers": Socializing the Quarry Landscape of the Wadi Hammamat', *Cambridge Archaeological Journal* 25/4 (2015), p. 797; and, for regular updates on work at the site, see <www.wadi-hammamat-project.co.uk>.

Chapter 3: History

For the history of ancient Egypt see Ian Shaw (ed.), *The Oxford History of Ancient Egypt* (Oxford, 2000) and Marc Van De Mieroop, *A History of Ancient Egypt* (Oxford, 2011). There are many different sources for the chronology of ancient Egypt, but four that provide very different perspectives on the way in which the dating system has been constructed from an elaborate combination of astronomical observations, king-lists, and genealogies are Richard Parker, *The Calendars of Ancient Egypt* (Chicago, 1950); Donald Redford, *Pharaonic King-lists, Annals and Day-Books: A Contribution to the Egyptian Sense of History* (Mississauga, 1986); Erik Hornung, Rolf Krauss, and David Warburton (eds), *Ancient Egyptian Chronology* (Leiden, 2006); and Andrew Shortland and Christopher Bronk Ramsey (eds), *Radiocarbon and the Chronologies of Ancient Egypt* (Oxford, 2013). For the ancient Egyptians' own sense of history see John Tait (ed.), *'Never had the Like Occurred': Egypt's View of its Past* (London, 2003), and John Baines, 'History and Historiography in the Material World: Ancient Egyptian Perspectives', in John Baines, Henriette van der Blom, Yi Samuel Chen, and Tim Rood (eds), *Historical Consciousness and the Use of the Past in the Ancient World* (Sheffield, 2019), pp. 109–32.

For an influential theory concerning the likely historical significance of late Predynastic votive mace-heads and palettes, see Nicholas

Millet, 'The Narmer Macehead and Related Objects', *Journal of the American Research Center in Egypt* 27 (1990), pp. 53–9.

For the ivory 'Narmer label' excavated by German archaeologists at Abydos in 2000, see Günter Dreyer, 'Egypt's Earliest Historical Event', *Egyptian Archaeology* 16 (2000), pp. 6–7. For the Palermo Stone, see Toby Wilkinson, *Royal Annals of Ancient Egypt* (London, 2000); for the Turin Papyrus, see Alan Gardiner, *The Turin Royal Canon* (Oxford, 1959) and Kim Ryholt, 'The Turin King List or So-called Royal Canon of Turin (TC) as a Source for Chronology', in Erik Hornung et al. (eds), *Ancient Egyptian Chronology* (Leiden, 2006), pp. 26–32; and for Manetho, see Gerald P. Verbrugghe and John M. Wickersham, *Berossos and Manetho, Introduced and Translated: Native Traditions in Ancient Mesopotamia and Egypt* (Ann Arbor, 2001).

For the controversy over the locations of astronomical observations used in Egyptian chronologies, see William Ward, 'The Present Status of Egyptian Chronology', *Bulletin of the American Schools of Oriental Research* 288 (1992), pp. 53–66, and for a recently discovered Old Kingdom heliacal observation of Sirius see M. E. Habicht, R. Gautschy, R. Siegmann, D. Rutica, and R. Hannig, 'A New Sothis Rise on a Small Cylindrical Jar from the Old Kingdom', *Göttinger Miszellen* 247 (2015), pp. 41–9. For seriation of coffins as a dating method, see Harco Willems, *Chests of Life: A Study of the Typology and Conceptual Development of Middle Kingdom Standard Class Coffins* (Leiden, 1988).

For the initial use of calibrated radiocarbon dates in Egyptian chronology see Ian Shaw, 'Egyptian Chronology and the Irish Oak Calibration', *Journal of Near Eastern Studies* 44 (1985), pp. 295–317, and for an excellent discussion of the current relationship between Egyptian history, building and radiocarbon dating, see Felix Hoflmayer, 'Radiocarbon Dating and Egyptian Chronology—From the "Curve of Knowns" to Bayesian Modelling', *Oxford Handbooks Online* (January 2016) [DOI: 10.1093/oxfordhb/9780199935413.013.64]. For successful recent projects applying radiocarbon dating to Egyptian history and prehistory, see Andrew Shortland and C. Bronk Ramsey (eds), *Radiocarbon and the Chronologies of Ancient Egypt* (Oxford, 2013) and Michael Dee et al., 'An Absolute Chronology for Early Egypt Using Radiocarbon Dating and Bayesian Statistical Modelling', *Proceedings of the Royal Society A* 469 (2013), 20130395.

Chapter 4: Writing

For studies of the hieroglyphic writing system, see Mark Collier and Bill Manley, *How to Read Hieroglyphs* (London, 1998); Penelope Wilson, *Sacred Signs* (Oxford, 2003); James Allen, *An Historical Study of Ancient Egyptian* (Cambridge, 2012); James Allen, *Middle Egyptian: An Introduction to the Language and Culture of Hieroglyphs* (Cambridge, 2014). There are several general collections of key Egyptian writings: Miriam Lichtheim, *Ancient Egyptian Literature*, 3 vols (Berkeley, 1973–80); Edward Wente, *Letters from Ancient Egypt* (Atlanta, 1990); Richard Parkinson, *Voices from Ancient Egypt* (London, 1991). Discussions of the methods of interpreting and analysing Egyptian texts include Antonio Loprieno (ed.), *Ancient Egyptian Literature: History and Forms* (Leiden, 1996) and Chris Eyre, *The Use of Documents in Pharaonic Egypt* (Oxford, 2013). Papyri and ostraca, particularly of the Roman period, are discussed by Roger S. Bagnall, *Reading Papyri, Writing Ancient History* (London, 1995). For the decipherment of hieroglyphs see Richard Parkinson, *Cracking Codes: The Rosetta Stone and Decipherment* (London, 1999), and (for Mesoamerican comparison and contrast) see also Michael Coe, *Breaking the Maya Code* (London, 1992).

For the origins of Egyptian writing, see Nicholas Postgate, Tao Wang, and Toby Wilkinson, 'The Evidence for Early Writing: Utilitarian or Ceremonial?', *Antiquity* 69 (1995), pp. 459–80; Frank Kammerzell, 'Old Egyptian and Pre-Old Egyptian: Tracing Linguistic Diversity in Archaic Egypt and the Creation of the Egyptian Language', in Stephan Seidlmayer (ed.), *Texte und Denkmäler des ägyptischen Alten Reiches* (Berlin, 2005), pp. 165–247; and David Wengrow, 'The Invention of Writing in Egypt', in Emily Teeter (ed.), *Before the Pyramids: The Origins of Egyptian Civilization* (Chicago, 2011), pp. 99–103.

Chapter 5: Kingship

For general discussions of Egyptian kingship see Henri Frankfort, *Kingship and the Gods* (Chicago, 1948); H. W. Fairman, 'The Kingship Rituals of Egypt', in Samuel H. Hooke (ed.), *Myth, Ritual and Kingship* (Oxford, 1958), pp. 74–104; David O'Connor and David Silverman (eds), *Ancient Egyptian Kingship* (Leiden, 1995), pp. 185–217. For Ptolemaic kingship, see Ellen E. Rice, *The Grand*

Procession of Ptolemy Philadelphus (Oxford, 1983); Klaus Bringmann, 'The King as Benefactor: Some Remarks on Ideal Kingship in the Age of Hellenism', in Anthony Bulloch, Erich S. Gruen, A. A. Long, and Andrew Stewart (eds), *Images and Ideologies: Self-Definition in the Hellenistic World* (Berkeley and London, 1993). The debate concerning coregencies can be explored in William Murnane, *Ancient Egyptian Coregencies* (Chicago, 1977) and David Lorton, 'Terms of Coregency in the Middle Kingdom', *Varia Aegyptiaca* 2 (1986), pp. 113–20.

For Amenhotep II, see Peter der Manuelian, *Studies in the Reign of Amenophis II* (Hildesheim, 1987) and Charles Van Siclen III, *Two Monuments from the Reign of Amenhotep II* (San Antonio, 1982) and *The Alabaster Shrine of King Amenhotep II* (San Antonio, 1986).

For Hatshepsut and Senenmut, see Suzanne Ratié, *La Reine Hatchepsout* (Leiden, 1979); Catharine H. Roehrig (ed.), with Renée Dreyfus and Cathleen A. Keller, *Hatshepsut: From Queen to Pharaoh* (New York and New Haven, 2005); and Peter Dorman, *The Monuments of Senenmut* (London, 1988) and *The Tombs of Senenmut: The Architecture and Decoration of Tombs 71 and 353* (New York, 1991).

For Ramesses II see Kenneth Kitchen, *Pharaoh Triumphant: The Life and Times of Ramesses II, King of Egypt*, 3rd edn (Warminster, 1985); Labib Habachi, *Features of the Deification of Ramesses II* (Glückstadt, 1969); and Joyce Tyldesley, *Ramesses: Egypt's Greatest Pharaoh* (London, 2000).

Chapter 6: Identity

For the theory concerning possible depiction of kite-like enclosures on the Narmer Palette, see Yigael Yadin, 'The Earliest Record of Egypt's Military Penetration into Asia?', *Israel Exploration Journal* 5/1 (1955), pp. 1–16, and, for more general discussion of evidence for early Egyptian contacts with Syria–Palestine, see Eliot Braun, 'South Levantine Early Bronze Age Chronological Correlations with Egypt in Light of the Narmer Serekhs from Tel Erani and Arad: New Interpretations', *British Museum Studies in Ancient Egypt and Sudan* 13 (2009), pp. 25–48.

For the DNA analysis suggesting increased sub-Saharan genetic links in modern Egyptians, see Verena Schuenemann, Alexander Peltzer, and Beatrix Welte, 'Ancient Egyptian Mummy Genomes Suggest an Increase of Sub-Saharan African Ancestry in Post-Roman

Periods', *Nature Communications* 8 (2017) [open access: <https://www.nature.com/articles/ncomms15694>].

For discussion of issues of Egyptian race and ethnicity, see Martin Bernal, *Black Athena: The Afro-Asiatic Roots of Classical Civilization*, 3 vols (London, 1987–2006); and for critiques of Bernal's controversial views, see Mary R. Lefkowitz and Guy M. Roberts (eds), *Black Athena Revisited* (Chapel Hill, NC, and London, 1996); and Wim van Binsbergen (ed.), *Black Athena Comes of Age* (Berlin, 2011). For a more general response to Afrocentrism, see Tunde Adeleke, *The Case Against Afrocentrism* (Jackson, Miss., 2009). Flinders Petrie's racist views on Egyptians are discussed by Debbie Challis in *The Archaeology of Race: The Eugenic Ideas of Francis Galton and Flinders Petrie* (New York and London, 2013).

For gender studies in Egyptology, see Gay Robins, *Women in Ancient Egypt* (London, 1993); Dorothea Arnold, *The Royal Women of Amarna* (New York, 1996); and K. Cooney, *When Women Ruled the World: Six Queens of Egypt* (Washington, DC, 2018). For sexuality, see Dominic Montserrat, *Sex and Society in Graeco-Roman Egypt* (London, 1996); Tom Hare, *ReMembering Osiris* (Stanford, Calif., 1999); and Carolyn Graves-Brown (ed.), *Sex and Gender in Ancient Egypt* (Swansea, 2008).

For Egyptian same-sex desire, see Richard Parkinson, '"Homosexual" Desire and Middle Kingdom Literature', *Journal of Egyptian Archaeology* 81 (1995), pp. 57–76, and, for homosexuality in the myth of Horus and Seth, see J. G. Griffiths, *The Conflict of Horus and Seth from Egyptian and Classical Sources* (Liverpool, 1960), 41–6. For the erotic sketch in a tomb above Hatshepsut's mortuary temple, see Christine Hue-Arce, 'Les Graffiti érotiques de la tombe 504 de Deir el-Bahari revisités', *Bulletin de l'Institut Français d'Archéologie Orientale* 113 (2013), pp. 193–202. Greg Reeder discusses 'Queer Egyptologies of Niankhkhnum and Khnumhotep', in Carolyn Graves-Brown (ed.), *Sex and Gender in Ancient Egypt* (Swansea, 2008), pp. 143–55, but note that opinion is still very divided on this topic.

Chapter 7: Death

For Osiris, see Tom Hare, *ReMembering Osiris* (Stanford, Calif., 1999) and Mark Smith, *Following Osiris: Perspectives on the Osirian Afterlife from Four Millennia* (Oxford, 2017). There is no shortage of books on death and mummification in ancient Egypt: examples include John Taylor, *Death and the Afterlife in Ancient Egypt* (London, 2001); Arthur C. Aufderheide, *The Scientific Study of Mummies* (Cambridge, 2003); Rosalie David (ed.), *Egyptian Mummies and Modern Science* (Cambridge and New York, 2008); and Mark Lehner and Zahi Hawass, *Giza and the Pyramids* (Chicago, 2017).

For the Predynastic mummies at Hierakonpolis, see Jana Jones, 'New Perspectives on the Development of Mummification and Funerary Practices during the Pre- and Early Dynastic Periods', in J.-C. Goyon and C. Cardin (eds), *Proceedings of the Ninth International Congress of Egyptologists* (Leuven, 2007), pp. 979–90. For the Neolithic experimental mummification see Jana Jones et al., 'Evidence for Prehistoric Origins of Egyptian Mummification in Late Neolithic Burials', *Public Library of Science ONE* 9/8 (2014), e103608. Regarding the Late Period embalming workshop at Saqqara, see Ramadan Hussein and Sylvie Marchand, 'A Mummification Workshop in Saqqara: The Pottery from the Main Shaft K24 (Saqqara Saite Tombs Project)', *Bulletin de Liaison de la Céramique Égyptienne* 29 (2019), pp. 101–32.

For the 'mummy's curse', see R. Luckhurst, *The Mummy's Curse: The True History of a Dark Fantasy* (Oxford, 2012). See also Nicholas Daly, 'That Obscure Object of Desire: Victorian Commodity Culture and Fictions of the Mummy', *NOVEL: A Forum on Fiction* 28 (1994), 24–51, for an interpretation of the popularity of mummy tales in Victorian and Edwardian times.

Chapter 8: Religion

Some earlier works on Egyptian religion and ideology are still important, e.g. Henri Frankfort, *Kingship and the Gods* (Chicago, 1948) and Siegfried Morenz, *Egyptian Religion* (London, 1973), but the best of the works published over the last thirty years are: Erik Hornung, *Idea into Image: Essays on Ancient Egyptian Thought* (New York, 1992); Geraldine Pinch, *Egyptian Myth: A Very Short Introduction* (Oxford, 2004); Emily Teeter, *Religion and Ritual in Ancient Egypt* (Cambridge, 2011); and Stephen Quirke, *Exploring Religion in Ancient Egypt* (Hassocks, 2015).

For discussion of the early monuments at Nabta Playa, see Fred Wendorf, Romuald Schild, and Nieves Zedeno, 'A Late Neolithic Megalith Complex in the Eastern Sahara: A Preliminary Report', in

Lech Krzyzaniak (ed.), *Interregional Contacts in the Later Prehistory of Northeastern Africa* (Poznan, 1996), pp. 125–32, and for the early temple at Hierakonpolis, see Reneé Friedman, 'Hierakonpolis Locality HK29A: The Predynastic Ceremonial Centre at Hierakonpolis Revisited', *Journal of the American Research Center in Egypt* 45 (2009), pp. 79–103. For comparable ritual areas at el-Mahsna and Naqada, see David Anderson, 'Zoomorphic Figurines from the Predynastic Settlement at el-Mahasna, Egypt', in Zahi Hawass and Janet Richards (eds), *The Archaeology and Art of Ancient Egypt* (Cairo, 2007), pp. 33–54, and Grazia Di Pietro, '"Kleinfunde" from the Italian Excavations at Zawaydah (Petrie's South Town)', in Hany Hanna (ed.), *The International Conference on Heritage of Naqada and Qus Region* (Cairo, 2007), pp. 79–87.

Chapter 9: Egyptomania

For a discussion of some of the theories concerning the nature and purpose of pyramids see Lynn Picknett and Clive Prince, 'Alternative Egypts', in Sally MacDonald and Michael Rice (eds), *Consuming Ancient Egypt* (London, 2003), pp. 175–94. For the idea of the pyramids being aligned with north via sighting of circumpolar stars, see Kate Spence, 'Ancient Egyptian Chronology and the Astronomical Orientation of the Pyramids', *Nature* 408 (2000), pp. 320–4. For Charles Piazzi Smyth's contribution to pyramidology, see *Life and Work at the Great Pyramid* (London, 1867).

For Akhenaten and the Amarna period see William Murnane, *Texts from the Amarna Period in Egypt* (Atlanta, 1995); Dominic Montserrat, *Akhenaten: History, Fantasy and Ancient Egypt* (London, 2000); Nicholas Reeves, *Akhenaten: Egypt's False Prophet* (London, 2001); Barry Kemp, *The City of Akhenaten and Nefertiti: Amarna and its People* (London, 2012); James K. Hoffmeier, *Akhenaten and the Origins of Monotheism* (Oxford, 2015). For discussion of the possibility of Nefertiti being buried in a hidden chamber of Tutankhamun's tomb, see C. N. Reeves, *The Burial of Nefertiti?*, Amarna Royal Tombs Project Occasional Paper 1: 1–16; and Jo Marchant, 'Is This Nefertiti's Tomb?', *Nature News* 20 Feb. 2020 (both available online).

For Nefertiti see Julia Samson, *Nefertiti and Cleopatra: Queen-Monarchs of Ancient Egypt* (London, 1985) and Joyce Tyldesley, *Nefertiti's Face: The Creation of an Icon* (London, 2018). For Cleopatra see Susan Walker and Peter Higgs, *Cleopatra of Egypt: From History to Myth* (London, 2001); Michel Chauveau, *Cleopatra: Beyond the Myth* (Ithaca, NY, 2002); Susan Walker and Sally-Ann Ashton, *Cleopatra Reassessed* (London, 2003); Joyce Tyldesley, *Cleopatra: Last Queen of Egypt* (London, 2009); Stacy Schiff, *Cleopatra: A Life* (New York, 2010); and Mary Hamer, *Signs of Cleopatra: Reading an Icon Historically* (Liverpool, 2014).

For a highly 'alternative' view of the Egyptian evidence, see Lynn Picknett and Clive Prince, *The Stargate Conspiracy: Revealing the Truth behind Extraterrestrial Contact, Military Intelligence and the Mysteries of Ancient Egypt* (London, 2000). For a fascinating spectrum of unconventional and innovative approaches to ancient Egypt see William Carruthers (ed.), *Histories of Egyptology: Interdisciplinary Measures* (New York, 2015).

Chapter 10: Cultural heritage

For discussion of the threats to Egyptian cultural heritage in the immediate aftermath of the Arab Spring, see articles by Monica Hanna and Salima Ikram in *Bulletin of the American Research Center in Egypt* 202 (2013), pp. 34–9, and *Journal of Mediterranean Archaeology & Heritage Studies* 1/4 (2013), pp. 366–75. For the failed sustainable heritage plan at the Temple of Khnum in Esna, see Marwa Ghanem and Samar Saad, 'Enhancing Sustainable Heritage Tourism in Egypt: Challenges and Framework of Action', *Journal of Heritage Tourism* 10/4 (2015), pp. 357–77, and for the unsuccessful strategies at Giza, see Ahemed Shetawy and Samah El Khateeb, 'The Pyramids Plateau: A Dream Searching for Survival', *Tourism Management* 30/6 (2009), pp. 819–27.

For cross-cultural views on the problems with Westernized approaches to Egyptian cultural heritage management, as well as some case-studies of fruitful current and future strategies, see Elizabeth Bloxam and Adel Kelany, 'Cultural Heritage Management in Egypt: Community-Based Strategies, Problems and Possibilities', in Ian Shaw and Elixabeth Bloxam (eds), *Oxford Handbook of Egyptology* (Oxford, 2020), pp. 232–51. For discussion of the current situation with museums and finds-stores in Egypt, see Maher A. Eissa and Ashraf el-Senussi, 'Egyptian Museums and Storehouses', also in the *Oxford Handbook of Egyptology*, pp. 1185–202. For a critique of the dearth of overall strategy behind the opening of new local museums in Egypt see Maher Eissa and Louay Saied, 'Museum Collections and Moving Objects in Egypt: An Approach to Amend the Current Situation', in Patrizia Piacentini et al. (eds), *Forming Material Egypt* (Milan, 2013), pp. 81–94. The website of the Grand Egyptian Museum, currently under construction at Giza, is <http://gem.gov.eg/index.htm>.

Index

For the benefit of digital users, indexed terms that span two pages (e.g., 52–53) may, on occasion, appear on only one of those pages.

Index

AFRICAN HISTORY
A Very Short Introduction
John Parker & Richard Rathbone

Essential reading for anyone interested in the African continent and the diversity of human history, this *Very Short Introduction* looks at Africa's past and reflects on the changing ways it has been imagined and represented. Key themes in current thinking about Africa's history are illustrated with a range of fascinating historical examples, drawn from over 5 millennia across this vast continent.

'A very well informed and sharply stated historiography...should be in every historiography student's kitbag. A tour de force...it made me think a great deal.'

Terence Ranger,
The Bulletin of the School of Oriental and African Studies

www.oup.com/vsi

BIBLICAL ARCHAEOLOGY
A Very Short Introduction
Eric H. Cline

Archaeologist Eric H. Cline here offers a complete overview of this exciting field. He discusses the early pioneers, the origins of biblical archaeology as a discipline, and the major controversies that first prompted explorers to go in search of sites that would "prove" the Bible. He then surveys some of the most well-known modern archaeologists, the sites that are essential sources of knowledge for biblical archaeology, and some of the most important discoveries that have been made in the last half century, including the Dead Sea Scrolls and the Tel Dan Stele.

www.oup.com/vsi

DRUIDS
A Very Short Introduction
Barry Cunliffe

The Druids first came into focus in Western Europe - Gaul, Britain, and Ireland - in the second century BC. They are a popular subject; they have been known and discussed for over 2,000 years and few figures flit so elusively through history. They are enigmatic and puzzling, partly because of the lack of knowledge about them has resulted in a wide spectrum of interpretations. Barry Cunliffe takes the reader through the evidence relating to the Druids, trying to decide what can be said and what can't be said about them. He examines why the nature of the druid caste changed quite dramatically over time, and how successive generations have interpreted the phenomenon in very different ways.

www.oup.com/vsi

ISLAMIC HISTORY
A Very Short Introduction
Adam J. Silverstein

Does history matter? This book argues not that history matters, but that Islamic history does. This *Very Short Introduction* introduces the story of Islamic history; the controversies surrounding its study; and the significance that it holds - for Muslims and for non-Muslims alike. Opening with a lucid overview of the rise and spread of Islam, from the seventh to twenty first century, the book charts the evolution of what was originally a small, localised community of believers into an international religion with over a billion adherents. Chapters are also dedicated to the peoples - Arabs, Persians, and Turks - who shaped Islamic history, and to three representative institutions - the mosque, jihad, and the caliphate - that highlight Islam's diversity over time.

'The book is extremely lucid, readable, sensibly organised, and wears its considerable learning, as they say, 'lightly'.'

BBC History Magazine

LATE ANTIQUITY
A Very Short Introduction
Gillian Clark

Late antiquity is the period (c.300–c.800) in which barbarian
invasions ended Roman Empire in Western Europe by the fifth
century and Arab invasions ended Roman rule over the
eastern and southern Mediterranean coasts by the seventh
century. Asking 'what, where, and when' Gillian Clark presents
an introduction to the concept of late antiquity and the events
of its time. Not only a period of cultural clashes, political
restructurings, and geographical controversies, Clark also
demonstrates the sheer richness and diversity of religious life
as well as the significant changes to trade, economy,
archaeology, and towns. Encapsulating significant
developments through vignettes, she reflects upon the period
by asking the question 'How much can we recognise in the
world of late antiquity?'

www.oup.com/vsi